WITHDRAWN

Also by Nathan Rabin

THE BIG REWIND:
A MEMOIR BROUGHT TO YOU BY POP CULTURE

MY YEAR OF FLOPS:
ONE MAN'S JOURNEY DEEP INTO THE
HEART OF CINEMATIC FAILURE

YOU
DON'T KNOW
ME BUT YOU
DON'T LIKE ME

Phish, Insane Clown Posse,
and My Misadventures with Two of
Music's Most Maligned Tribes

NATHAN RABIN

SCRIBNER

New York   London   Toronto   Sydney   New Delhi

SCRIBNER
A Division of Simon & Schuster, Inc.
1230 Avenue of the Americas
New York, NY 10020

First Scribner trade paperback edition June 2013

SCRIBNER and design are registered trademarks of The Gale Group, Inc.,
used under license by Simon & Schuster, Inc., the publisher of this work.

For information about special discounts for bulk purchases,
please contact Simon & Schuster Special Sales at 1-866-506-1949
or business@simonandschuster.com.

The Simon & Schuster Speakers Bureau can bring authors to your live event.
For more information or to book an event contact the Simon & Schuster Speakers
Bureau at 1-866-248-3049 or visit our website at www.simonspeakers.com.

Designed by Mspace/Maura Fadden Rosenthal

Manufactured in the United States of America

1   3   5   7   9   10   8   6   4   2

Library of Congress Control Number: 2013011702

ISBN 978-1-4516-2688-9
ISBN 978-1-4516-2690-2 (ebook)

For Keith and Stephen,
thanks for giving me a career to ruin with this book

CONTENTS

WHAT MADNESS HAVE I
GOTTEN MYSELF INTO?

t begins, as these things generally do, with a girl. When I was twenty-five years old in 2001 I traveled to Marietta, Georgia, to visit my younger sister, Shari, and became instantly enraptured with a radiant seventeen-year-old friend of hers I will call Cadence Caraway. Though we spent only an hour together having brunch, the memory of Cadence haunted me until eight years later when she contacted me on the message boards for the *A.V. Club,* the entertainment monolith where I have toiled as head writer since the beginning of time. We fell in love via e-mails and phone conversations before beginning a long-distance romance that found us shuttling back and forth between Providence, Rhode Island, where Cadence was getting her master's in teaching from Brown, and my hometown of Chicago.

In Providence one of our most beloved and oft-repeated rituals entailed compulsively watching the music video for "Miracles," from controversial Detroit horrorcore duo Insane Clown Posse. We were mesmerized by the surreal incongruity between the gothic artifice of Insane Clown Posse's wicked-clown persona and the video's glorious lack of self-consciousness. The self-styled World's Most Hated Group had been on the periphery of my consciousness since I started writing about pop culture for the *A.V. Club.* The band was an easy punch line for cynics, as well as the inspiration for the most mocked and reviled subculture in existence: Juggalos, the strange, often Midwestern creatures who wore clown makeup, greeted each other with hearty cries of "Whoop whoop," "Family," and "Magic magic ninja what!" and sprayed themselves with off-brand Faygo sodas during concerts rich in theatricality and homemade spectacle. They unite every year for an infamous multiday bacchanal known as the Gathering of the Juggalos.

Deans of pop culture had treated the duo with equal parts fascination and repulsion, but after "Miracles" my mild curiosity about Insane Clown Posse and the wild, weird, disreputable world they rule as clown-painted demon deities evolved into something more serious. Yet even as someone fortunate enough to be able to write about his obsessions for a living, I had only a fuzzy conception of what a massive role Insane Clown Posse (aka ICP) and especially their passionate, intense, and unique fans would play in the next few years of my life.

Cadence shared my intense obsession with "Miracles" even if the duo's self-deprecating, tongue-in-cheek take on horrorcore couldn't have been further from her usual tastes. In one of her first e-mails to me, Cadence inquired, "Do you like the band Phish?" I freaked out a little bit. Asking someone if they like Phish is a loaded question. It's not like asking, "Do you like Squeeze?" Nobody is liable to care if you enjoy the music of the veteran British pop band behind "Tempted" and "Pulling Mussels from a Shell," but if someone says they're really into Phish, we're often tempted to make sweeping generalizations about their personality, intelligence, personal hygiene, sobriety, class, education, and taste.

There's a great T-shirt from my employers at the *Onion* that reads, STEREOTYPES ARE A REAL TIME-SAVER. That's certainly true when it comes to Phish and Insane Clown Posse. Buy into the stereotype of Juggalos as uneducated, violent, racist, and ignorant, or Phish fans as unemployed, weed-smoking, unjustifiably privileged space cadets, and you don't have to waste time listening to their music or actually interacting with any of their fans.

Part of the revulsion people feel toward Phish and Insane Clown Posse is physical in nature. Being a hardcore Insane Clown Posse fan is an intensely visceral experience involving sticky clown makeup, soda-soaked clothing, homemade tattoos, and, in the case of the Gathering of the Juggalos, thousands of Juggalos gathering in a remote, drug-sex-and-alcohol-choked rural environment for days on end with extraordinarily limited access to showers, toiletries, and other niceties. On a primal level, a lot of people find Juggalos just plain gross.

Phish fans aren't held in the same contempt, in part because their fan base tends to be better educated and wealthier than the overwhelmingly working-class Juggalos, but as the biggest and best-known jam band in existence, Phish is one of the primary targets of our culture's long-standing antihippie bias. By the time I went to college in Madison, Wisconsin, in 1994, Phish was *the* hippie band, just as the Grateful Dead was *the* hippie band for generations before it. Like the Grateful Dead, Phish tends to be judged by the culture and attitudes of its fans as much as the content of its music. As a college kid, I came to see Phish as the band whose music you were casually forced to listen to in exchange for a free bowl of pot. I don't remember the music nearly as much as I remember those experiences. I think that's true for a lot of people's perception of Phish: The music floats away into a noodly, interchangeable blur of guitar solos and free-form sonic experimentation, but the stoned grins, tie-dyed shirts, and mellow vibes of fans linger on. In part because its oeuvre was critically unfashionable and terminally unhip, I let Phish's music wash over me without really thinking about it or really, truly listening to it.

As I grew older I internalized our culture's revisionist take on hippies as drug-addicted, myopic brats luxuriating in eternal adolescence. I inherited the widespread sense that hippies were getting away with something, that they were lazily opting out of civilization to get high in a field while the grueling machinery of late-period capitalism continued without them.

The hippie ethos and Phish's mythology are inextricably intertwined: Phish isn't a band; it's a way of life. It's a name that conjures up images of lost children with scruffy beards and tie-dyed shorts and sad, emaciated pit bulls on rope chains accompanied by dreadlocked white women habitually clad in flowing dresses.

"Do you like the band Phish?" implicitly means, "How do you feel about jam bands? How do you feel about people who follow Phish? How do you feel about marijuana and Ecstasy and nitrous and acid and mushrooms? How do you feel about traveling from town to town and devoting your life to the music of a group of middle-aged men? How do you feel about the Grateful Dead? How do you feel about the sixties? How do you feel about sex and freedom and the liberating powers of rock 'n' roll? How do you feel about the open road? How do you feel about earnestness and sincerity and sneering, protective irony?"

Did I like the band Phish? I had no idea. I'd lazily bought into the overriding cultural assessment of the band and its fans, but now I had a whole new frame of reference: my beloved Cadence.

Phish had made my Cadence happy. I wanted to be part of anything that gave her joy. I fell in love with her in a way that paradoxically made me feel powerful and powerless, bulletproof and vulnerable. I felt like I could accomplish anything with her by my side but the prospect of losing her terrified me. I didn't just want to be her present and future: I wanted to retroactively become her past as well. I wanted to somehow Photoshop myself into her memories. I wanted to travel back in time and twirl ecstatically at half-forgotten festivals. I fell in love with the woman Cadence had become but I was also in love with the beautiful child she had been. Maybe that's what my sudden urge to see as many Phish shows as possible was ultimately about: rewriting Cadence's history with me as the romantic lead.

How could I hold on to my knee-jerk anti-Phish prejudice when the band meant so much to the greatest source of happiness in my life? As a freakishly smart, preternaturally verbal, obscenely well-read teenager in the sprawling suburban wasteland of Marietta, Georgia (Newt Gingrich's district), Cadence followed Phish to escape a dispiriting universe of jocks and skinny blonde girls, a soul-crushingly homogenous realm where everyone became a real estate salesman or stockbroker, got married in their early twenties, voted Republican, and traded lawn-maintenance tips at the country club after work. To Cadence, Phish fandom was a way of both asserting her individuality and joining a tribe.

Though we grew up nearly a decade apart and several universes away from each other, we both sought out books and music and movies and ideas as a way of escaping a world where we didn't belong. For me, that meant throwing myself into art that expressed the bottomless rage I felt. I lost myself in the anarchic anger of Johnny Rotten or the righteous rebellion of the Coup. For Cadence, it meant traveling in the opposite direction, seeking out music and a scene that stumbled toward grace, toward transcendence, toward the eternal ideal of one nation under a groove.

We are born with open minds. We want to explore, to learn, to grow, to see and experience everything. But as we get older our minds begin to close. We become stuck in our ways. Preferences become prejudices. Yes, yes, yes is replaced by Bartleby's "I'd prefer not to." New movements and stars and genres strike us as strange, incomprehensible, objectionable, and ridiculous. Our lust for knowledge and adventure is replaced by a desire for those damned kids to get off our lawn and turn down that crazy jungle music while they're at it. We fetishize the music and movies and movements of our youth. We retreat into the comforting cocoon of the familiar.

After a lifetime of feeling different, I started to wonder if we're all secretly the same. I began to suspect that what divides us isn't as important as what unites us. We all hurt and ache and bleed and struggle and love. We just listen to different music and align ourselves with different subcultures while we do so.

Like Phish, Insane Clown Posse has developed a vast, intensely loyal grassroots following despite being alternately ignored and mocked by the mainstream. In the case of Insane Clown Posse at least, it could be argued that the group has an intensely loyal grassroots following *because* it has been alternately ignored and mocked by the mainstream, not despite it. As Insane Clown Posse's Violent J likes to say, the colder it is outside the circle, the warmer it is inside. The sense of persecution many Juggalos feel from the outside world serves to bind them closer together.

The parallels between the seemingly antithetical groups are

legion. They each have elaborate homemade mythologies. Phish has its "Gamehenge" song cycle, a dense, C. S. Lewis/J. R. R. Tolkien–style saga of good and evil rooted in *The Man Who Stepped into Yesterday*, a concept album frontman Trey Anastasio wrote as his senior study while enrolled in Goddard College in the mid-1980s.

The Man Who Stepped into Yesterday chronicles the fantastical adventures of an aging military man named Colonel Forbin who finds a door into the mythical realm of Gamehenge, a world populated by the Lizards, a peaceful people who led an idyllic existence dictated by the precepts of a manual called the Helping Friendly Book before an evil outsider named Wilson took advantage of their trusting nature to enslave them using knowledge gleaned from the book, which he had hidden away to keep the Lizards from harnessing its incredible power. Colonel Forbin tries to retrieve the Helping Friendly Book to aid the Lizards in their rebellion against the nefarious Wilson, only to have it fall into the hands of a character named Errand Wolfe, who uses it to overthrow Wilson and install himself as ruler instead of returning the book to the Lizards. In *The Man Who Stepped into Yesterday*, as in life, power corrupts and absolute power corrupts absolutely. Phish has never released *The Man Who Stepped into Yesterday* as a studio album but its songs, characters, and conflicts live on in the band's regular live performances of songs from the opus.

Insane Clown Posse has an even more convoluted and central mythology involving the afterlife collectively known as the Dark Carnival, rooted in a series of "Joker's Cards" that correspond to different ICP albums.

Insane Clown Posse and Phish have both worked to cultivate a sense of community with their followers that obliterates the distinction between artist and fan.

But more than elaborate mythologies, Phish and Insane Clown Posse offer fans the sense of community, identity, and belonging that comes with joining a tight-knit if widely disparaged tribe with its own set of rituals, traditions, and homemade folklore. When I examine my soul, I have to admit that this sense of community and belonging probably attracted me to Phish and Insane Clown Posse as much as the fascinating place they hold in pop culture.

To research the curious ways of modern musical tribes, I decided to augment my travels to Hallowicked and the Gathering of the Juggalos by following Phish with Cadence throughout the summer of 2010. When that proved an epic boondoggle, I found myself heading out on the road to follow Phish in the summer of 2011 in a radically different, perilous new context: I was now broke, desperate, half mad, terrified that my world was about to be rent asunder at any moment, and, most dramatically of all, without Cadence.

You Don't Know Me but You Don't Like Me is the rambling tale of a man who followed Phish and Insane Clown Posse for two years and lost his way, whose mind and mission got hopelessly scrambled somewhere along the glorious, hazardous road, and who just barely managed to crawl his way back home. It is a much different book from the tidy, anthropological tome I set out to write, but it's also the only book I could have written honestly and with a clear conscience. I set out to write a book about musical fandom from the outside in. Instead I ended up writing a book about fandom from the inside out.

What could have motivated me to devote my summers to a band and subculture that had been so utterly foreign to me? Love plays a central role, but I also wanted to capture a snapshot of a funky subsection of the pop-culture universe. I wanted to do it before age and responsibility made traveling across the country to follow a rock 'n' roll band impossible, before I *really* had to grow up. I didn't realize when I began that I had already passed that point in my life and that every time I headed out on the road, I did so at my own peril.

I wanted to understand what attracts people like my beloved Cadence to the traveling carnival of a Phish tour. What compelled others to paint their faces like clowns and get tattoos of Hatchetman, the mascot for ICP's Psychopathic label? I wanted to delve beyond the caricature of jam-band fans and horror-core scrubs. I decided to throw myself on the front lines of first-person journalistic experimentation, like Barbara Ehrenreich in *Nickel and Dimed* or David Foster Wallace munching on a corn dog at the state fair or A. J. Jacobs dressing up like Moses or that book where George Plimpton went undercover with the Symbionese Liberation Army and ended up offing all those pigs.

My curious years following two of the strangest and strongest musical subcultures represented my first and last fling. Throughout my twenties I avoided many of the responsibilities of adulthood out of a delusional conviction that I'd wake up one day and be transformed into a young Jack Kerouac. I'd become a drifter, a gypsy, an upscale hobo, the Wandering Jew, a merry prankster, a good old American guest. A man like that cannot and should not be tied down by a mortgage, marriage, and fatherhood. As Billy Joe Shaver reminds us, doers and thinkers say moving is the closest thing to being free. As an American, I have an inalienable right to pretend that I'm perpetually on the verge of throwing it all away and heading out onto the open road. I cherish that illusion. Or at least I did until it smashed up hard against a brick wall of reality.

STEPPING INTO TOMORROW:
PHISH IN MIAMI, 2009

Before jetting around North America as an amateur pop-culture anthropologist, I wanted to test the waters by attending three Phish shows in Miami on December 29, 30, and 31, 2009. For months those dates loomed in my mind as half promise and half threat. Would I really go through with it? Was it masochistic for me to commit myself to watching at least nine hours of a band I'd never listened to of my own accord? What was I trying to prove? Who was I trying to prove it to? Was this a strange dare I would come to regret? Or did I really just need to get the fuck over myself? (The answer to that last question, incidentally, is yes.)

Cadence and I arrived in Miami around five o'clock on the 29th following a twelve-hour car ride from Marietta, exhausted and unbelievably excited in equal measures. In front of our dumpy yet charming hotel a pair of scruffy young men wandered about in cargo shorts and flip-flops. It felt redundant when Cadence asked them if they were in town for the show. It was not difficult to differentiate between the out-of-towners and the townies reluctantly tolerating their presence. At the front desk you could cut the class tension with a knife, as a Cuban clerk did little to mask his contempt for the stoned tourists stumbling around his hotel.

The members of Phish weren't exactly descended from hobos or sharecroppers. Frontman Trey Anastasio's father was an executive at the testing company behind the SAT and GRE and his mother an editor at *Sesame Street Magazine*. Keyboardist Page McConnell's father was one of the inventors of Tylenol. Drummer Jon Fishman and bassist Mike Gordon come from similarly solid suburban backgrounds. After hooking up in Vermont in the mid-eighties, Phish flourished in the womblike warmth and comfort of a supportive local college-music scene.

The band's genre-bending, whimsical, and psychedelic songs transformed fans into musical evangelists who spread the gospel through bootlegs delivered with passionate testimonials to the group's greatness along with caveats that said greatness could only truly be understood watching them perform live, preferably while stoned on one or more mind-altering substances. Every generation must assert its independence and autonomy by rejecting the music of the generations that came before them. For a lot of early Phish fans, the Grateful Dead represented the music and mind-set of their fathers and uncles and older brothers. The Grateful Dead was something they inherited; Phish was something they could claim as their own. It belonged to them.

Critics tended to analyze Phish's fan base more than its music. The typical review was a Mad Libs–like construction littered with Grateful Dead references, snarky comments about fans perpetually encircled in a cloud of pot smoke like Pigpen from *Peanuts*, and complaints about noodly jams and endless guitar solos.

Phish fulfilled few of the requirements of musical stardom: They made exactly one music video (for "Down with Disease"), they weren't particularly good-looking, and they actively avoided having a hit single.

Phish fans have a tendency to fetishize and romanticize the early years, when the scene was small and hermetic enough to feel like one big extended family. People became fans because they'd had a quasi-religious, semiorgasmic revelation after going to a show or being given a bootleg by a friend, not because they'd read about them in a magazine or kept hearing that one song on their drive home from work. The band created a secret language for fans, a homegrown vernacular of in-jokes, running gags, slang, and interactive bits. Phish varied its set list every night and made legal downloads of shows available almost immediately on its website. They were a jam band for an online era whose big Internet presence served to blur the line separating hippies from geeks.

For a lot of fans,1996 marked the end of an era. It was the year the world found out about a band that had previously been their little secret. The group recorded *Billy Breathes* with superproducer Steve Lillywhite (U2, Morrissey) and watched the album debut in the top ten. The spare, unrelentingly melodic *Billy Breathes* is an album of powerful quiet: It doesn't shout its greatness from the mountaintops so much as it whispers its modest, insinuating charms. It's also very transparently an effort to make a real album of tight, concise pop songs rather than compiling ramshackle vehicles for onstage jamming. The year 1996 similarly marked the first of a series of festivals that consolidated Phish's reputation as a major countercultural force. On August 16 and 17, Phish played to seventy thousand fans—making it the biggest rock concert in the country that year—at a former air force base in Plattsburgh, New York, for an event called The Clifford Ball.

The festivals grew in ambition until, as 1999 turned to 2000, at a festival called Big Cypress, Phish played a seven-and-a-half-hour New Year's Eve set that lasted from just after midnight on New Year's Eve to sunrise New Year's Day. It was widely considered the greatest Phish show of all time and the apex of the band's career. Phish had become so huge the media was forced to acknowledge it. Its members made the cover of *Entertainment Weekly* in 2000 and the Big Cypress show was covered by Peter Jennings on ABC's *World News Tonight*.

Phish had hit the pinnacle. There was nowhere to go but down. That's just where it headed, with a vengeance. In *Boogie Nights,* a New Year's Eve party on the dawn of 1980 marks the moment when everything good turns bad and the formerly charmed characters' momentum begins spinning violently, madly, uncontrollably in the wrong direction. The drugs stop being fun and desperation takes hold.

That was Big Cypress for Phish. The death of Jerry Garcia in 1995 had brought an influx of opportunistic Deadheads into the scene along with cocaine, heroin, and meth. Hard drugs pervaded the private world of Phish as well. Anastasio threw himself into partying with the same pummeling intensity he brought to leading Phish and becoming one of the greatest guitar players in the world.

Phish became a prisoner of its success, no longer a band but a huge commercial enterprise with a massive infrastructure to support, from the road crew to an ever-increasing home office that handled a wide variety of services in-house. In 2000 Phish took a two-year hiatus. In 2004, following a disastrous Las Vegas stint, Anastasio shocked fans by announcing that the band would be breaking up.

As for the band itself, Page McConnell supported the measure, but Mike Gordon made no secret of his opposition to the breakup. Anastasio had destroyed the world he'd created. Diehards had made the band their life. Now that life was over. Fans felt stranded and betrayed. Had they been worshipping at the altar of a false god?

Yet, remarkably, the worst was yet to come. In 2004 Anastasio was bottoming out both personally and professionally. When the nucleus of an entire lifestyle is blasted out of his mind on heroin, booze, coke, and pills, it's bound to have a ripple effect.

The band's final festival in Coventry, Vermont, in 2004 proved a logistical nightmare. Due to a combination of poor planning, torrential rain, and miscommunication, a traffic jam ensued that was so brutal fans parked their cars in the middle of the muddy road and walked to the venue on foot. The *New York Times* quoted Fishman calling the band's final shows at Coventry "one of the great train wrecks in live concert history."

In 2006 Anastasio was arrested for possession of Xanax, Percocet, hydrocodone, and heroin and driving while intoxicated. He spent fourteen months in a drug-treatment program. As part of his community service, he was required to clean fairgrounds and scour toilets.

As Anastasio told Congress while advocating for treatment of drug offenders rather than jail, "My life had become a catastrophe. I had no idea how to turn it around. My band had broken up. I had almost lost my family. My whole life had devolved into a disaster. I believe that the police officer who stopped me at three A.M. that morning saved my life."

Following Phish meant escape and freedom from responsibility to its acolytes. Being the frontman for Phish meant something much different to Anastasio. Being the epicenter of an entire subculture proved an almost unbearable burden, just as it had hastened Garcia's smack-addled lurch to an early grave. Uneasy lies the head that wears the crown. The entire Phish phenomenon rested unsteadily on Anastasio's slumped shoulders. Everyone was depending on him. Eventually he wilted under the pressure. He was at the core of a scene where drugs were less a recreational activity or a way to unwind than a lifestyle, an end unto themselves.

Then in 2009 a clean and sober Anastasio reunited with the rest of Phish and the great beast rose from its five-year slumber to the delight of the subculture that had mourned its demise like the death of a loved one. By that time a lot of their fan base had grown up and moved on, like my Cadence. By then Phish was a fading memory that connected her to a world she used to know and the beautiful child she used to be.

Before the concert in Miami that first night, I experienced my first taste of what Phish fans call the Lot, one of many traditions the band's fans imported wholesale from Grateful Dead fans, though Deadheads called their version Shakedown Street, after a Dead song. It's a stadium parking lot where stereotypes come to life in vivid Technicolor; rotting vans, shaggy men and women with dilated pupils and vacant expressions, sad little makeshift stands selling questionable-looking burritos and other foodstuffs. But more than anything, the Lot is an open-air drug market, a traveling swap meet for mood-altering substances.

It was in the Lot that I took nitrous oxide for the first time. Cadence had told me that taking a hit of nitrous was like getting punched in the face repeatedly, but in a good way; a huge, almost overpowering rush that dissipated almost instantly. It was not the world's greatest sales pitch, but I'll take anything that won't destroy me, so I purchased three balloons pumped full of nitrous from what I'm sure was a reputable vendor, untied the balloons, inhaled deeply, and waited for a wave of euphoria to wash over me. But all I felt was a mild light-headedness. It was pleasant and goofy, but it wasn't anywhere near as intense as promised.

Maybe that was for the best, for throughout the week I came across hippies sprawled on the ground, their eyes glassy and empty, an idiot grin of stupefied satisfaction on their ecstatic faces and used balloons scattered at their feet. They looked like revelers at a birthday party for the world's most debauched eight-year-old. I found this juxtaposition of childhood innocence and adult excess deeply disturbing. The people on nitrous oxide looked so sloppy and fucked up, so out of control, so unencumbered by dignity or self-consciousness.

I pitied these sad, jubilant creatures, these sentient puddles of naked hedonism. I felt bad for them. I judged them harshly. And I envied them. Part of me wanted to call up their parents and part of me wished that I, too, could lie on the ground in a fucked-up haze without worrying what people thought of me.

We tend to process subcultures that way. We're horrified by a funky subsection of society's loose morals, chemical dependencies, lack of self-discipline, garish garb, and unconscionable hairstyles. But more than anything, we're terrified that these people who have nothing in common with us, who sneer insouciantly at our values and way of life, are having more fun than we are. We can't join them, so we beat them up with our words and attitudes.

During a book tour for my 2009 memoir, *The Big Rewind*, a jarhead chauffeur drove me from Milwaukee to Madison. He was a fifth-generation military man whose life revolved around God, country, and cars, the kind of true believer who has an official-looking portrait of George W. Bush as the screen saver for his cell phone, and not in an ironic way. He was so militantly polite and formal that he would apologize for using words like *darn* and *crap*. Though I suspect he would have found the book I was promoting, and every other aspect of my existence, deeply objectionable, I liked him a lot. He talked about driving a group of well-heeled Phish fans to a concert in a limousine and how they asked if they could toke up in the backseat. He told them it would be against regulations for them to smoke while he was in the vehicle but if they wanted to smoke while he went for a walk, that would be acceptable.

At the end of his anecdote he got a faraway look in his eyes and said, "I obviously don't approve of their lifestyle, but sometimes"—he paused, choosing his words carefully—"I wish that I could be like them."

Now I was living the chauffeur's secret fantasy. Watching Phish perform that first night, I realized that following them would entail changing the way I processed music. I've always been a lyrics guy. I gravitated to hip-hop, and, later, country because they tell good stories. But to my untrained ears, the lyrics in Phish's songs seemed irrelevant. They were doggerel, random silliness, free-floating whimsy, a means to an end, a framework for the solos and extended improvisation that was the real crux of their music. It wasn't about playing a hit song; it was about embarking on an open-ended sonic journey and taking a stadiumful of fellow travelers along for the ride.

There were compelling stories everywhere I looked, but they weren't necessarily found in Phish songs. It was the story of four men from Vermont who started a band that became a lifestyle and an institution. It was the story of Phish's relationship with their fans. It was the story of Phish's breakup and reunion. It was the story of a teenage Cadence finding a way out of Marietta. It was the story of lost kids flocking to a scene promising a sense of community and solidarity, and trust fund babies enjoying a few laughs before taking over Daddy's company. It was the story of a boy who so loved a girl that he would follow her through the gates of hell. It was the story of what Phish meant to Cadence as a dreadlocked teenage rebel and what they meant to her as a twenty-six-year-old.

It was a story of rebirth, renewal, and redemption. Cadence says that the vibe around Phish shows before the band broke up in 2004 had turned dark and sinister. An air of decadence permeated the scene, untethered to any political or social consciousness. It wasn't unusual to see a mother pushing a stroller while shouting, "Got coke, got meth, got E," or fans with big black bags under their eyes and a zombielike pallor stumbling out of a Porta-Potty clutching their wrists. I wanted to hear all of these stories, soak it all in, get outside myself and my hang-ups and neuroses. I wanted to tune in, turn on, and drop out.

I'd grown up thinking of rock and rap stars as gods who deigned to favor us with their genius. I went to concerts to worship pop, to prostrate myself before my larger-than-life heroes. Live performance was about sex, charisma, youth, hero worship, escape, and the unbridgeable gulf between rock god and worshipful fan.

I saw little of that during that first night in Miami. The band looked like adjunct professors at a small liberal arts college.

It's hard to get a sense of Phish as a band from its studio albums, since the songs serve primarily as rough outlines that can be fleshed out and expanded into dazzling new shapes in concert. Songs that last three and a half minutes in album form are massaged into ten-minute epics onstage, while ten-minute epics have been known to last weeks.

If I was going to make it through my Phish excursion, I'd have to repress my preference for short, punchy songs. I'd have to stop favoring energy and enthusiasm over technical virtuosity. I'd need to embrace the soloing, improvisation, free-floating whimsy, structural complexity, and goofball humor endemic to Phish's oeuvre. I would have to recalibrate the way I processed music and learn to listen in a new way. I would need to stop worrying and love the dreaded extended guitar solo.

That first night, I was introduced to songs that would come to mean a great deal to me, that in the years ahead would become filled with vivid Proustian associations of peoples and places and substances, like the popular set opener "Kill Devil Falls," which would become synonymous with travel, adventure, and the exhilarating rush of excitement that characterize the beginning of a Phish show in a new town, or the heartbreakingly pretty "Prince Caspian," whose lovely chorus—"Oh, to be Prince Caspian, afloat upon the waves"—captures the yearning for transcendence and escape coursing through so many Phish songs. Those and other songs would someday wind their way deep into my consciousness, but that first night they were just catchy songs that stood out from the pleasant haze of guitar solos and endless jams.

The next night I was, to quote *The Blues Brothers,* on a mission from God. I was going to buy and then take MDMA (the base component of Ecstasy), or "Molly," for the first time. The Lot was dirty, it was sordid, it was filled with illegal wares, and it was more than a little bit awesome. The Lot embodied all that was good and bad about the counterculture in microcosm. It was where Woodstock collided into Altamont, the wild party and the crushing hangover the next morning.

But we were not there as sociological observers. We were there to buy drugs. Cadence and I have vastly different ways of pursuing our objectives. Cadence does this bizarre thing where if she wants something, she goes after it. I prefer a more indirect approach. If I want something I'll think long and hard about how badly I want it, then try to wish it into existence with my mind.

Cadence and I pursued our antithetical strategies in the Lot. I silently wished someone would detect a "Hey, I would like to buy MDMA" look on our faces and offer us some, while Cadence purposefully strode around the Lot asking everyone within earshot, "Molly? Molly? We're looking for Molly! Does anyone have any Molly?"

Cadence's approach worked better than mine.

"Hey man, I've got some Molly," a wasted-looking young man in an outsize sweatshirt and baseball cap offered. "Sixty bucks."

Acting as my consigliere, Cadence offered him fifty.

"Nah man, it's gotta be—" the hapless drug dealer began, until his identically outfitted girlfriend entered the picture and brusquely demanded, "Take whatever you can get. Don't haggle."

I took the Molly, headed into the stadium, and waited for the magic to happen. Cadence makes a special point of never sitting in her assigned seat, so we moved up to a row farther down and sat next to a nice pair of bearded, overalls-wearing gentlemen who shared their stories with us. One of them enthused, "I'd never even been to a Phish show before a couple of days ago. I work at a gas station in Alabama and it's not hard to get time off. So when my buddy told me what a good time it was, I started going to shows. Now I'm practically addicted to it."

Taking the Molly had a subtle but tangible effect: It completely destroyed my ability to function in the world. Also, my brain stopped working. In my paranoid state, I became convinced that the nice young men sitting next to us would kidnap Cadence the second I was out of sight. When I got up to use the bathroom I remember thinking, "I really need to take a piss but if I leave I might never see Cadence again." Then again, I really did need to take a piss.

I detected a brief flash of panic dancing over Cadence's eyes as I left, perhaps for the very last time. "Hurry back soon!" she implored with a hint of desperation in her voice.

I made it to the bathroom all right, but I lost my shit immediately afterward. As I staggered back to the general vicinity of our seats, nothing made sense. Row 103 was followed by 104 and then 105. Fuck, what was that supposed to mean? Was there even a pattern to that random set of numbers?

My mind traveled to very dark places. I became convinced that the men sitting next to us dragged Cadence away from the arena by her long, luxurious hair, stuck her in the back of a van with the windows blacked out and a majestic wizard astride a unicorn painted on the side, and planned to take her back to Alabama so that she could become their shared wife. No! I couldn't let that happen. I had only myself to blame; if I didn't want Cadence to be kidnapped by deranged hillbillies, I never should have smoked that guy's pot. Or taken MDMA. Or gone to a crazy rock 'n' roll show. Or stopped going to synagogue after my parents got divorced.

Astonishingly, I made it back to my seat, next to Cadence, and recovered to an extent. The Molly I'd ingested gave the entire concert a tactile, sensual quality. I felt like I was somehow inside the music. The magic was happening. I never stopped smiling a big, goofy grin at Cadence once we were joyously reunited.

That night Phish played a ramshackle but ingratiating cover of "Dixie Cannonball," ambled its way through Taj Mahal's "Corrina," Argent's "Hold Your Head Up," the Edgar Winter Band's "Frankenstein," and "Boogie On Reggae Woman," a Stevie Wonder cover Phish should stay far away from on the basis of its title alone. Or so I thought. In time I'd come to love Phish's version of "Boogie On Reggae Woman" as pure, uninhibited, joyous liberation. I'd eagerly anticipate it. But that first weekend I held on to cynicism like a life preserver. I thought I needed it. I thought I needed my defenses. Time would prove me wrong. I wouldn't get anything of value out of my travels until I let myself go, until I abandoned a detached critical perspective and made a conscious decision to lose myself in the moment.

As a stranger to both the jam-band world and Phish, I appreciated how many covers the band plays: Their takes on "A Day in the Life" and songs from the Rolling Stones' *Exile on Main Street* instantly transported me to other realms of the pop-culture and musical world I knew and loved. They were comforting, soothing reminders that Phish's influences, frame of reference, and worldview extend far beyond the jam-band universe.

The jams were just as long and the lyrics as inscrutable that second night, but the MDMA did wonders for my attention span and concentration.

Cadence and I exited the show on the kind of natural high accessible only to people on illegal drugs. I had the woman I loved by my side and a mind full of strange and wonderful chemicals.

We floated in the general direction of our hotel, surfing a massive wave of good vibes. Tie-dyed and sandal-wearing space cadets surrounded us. We were all on the same wavelength, united in our righteous crusade for jam-band nirvana.

Then somewhere we made a wrong turn and found ourselves inexplicably alone on a desolate-looking street. One minute fellow travelers cocooned us. The next we appeared to have wandered into one of those ominous empty streets found in zombie movies.

The only vehicles we encountered were cop cars. Every time we'd see a car we'd lurch in its general direction, our pupils as big as dimes, our arms waving wildly and perhaps threateningly, as we begged the law enforcement officers for directions. They were, perhaps not surprisingly, a little freaked out. I couldn't tell if they were giving bad directions or if we were just too fucked up to follow them correctly.

Finally Cadence pleaded with one of the cops, "We're really, really lost and have no idea where our hotel is. If you could just give us a ride to our hotel we would be *sooooo* appreciative. It should just be five or six blocks from here."

The cop glared at us with a faintly disgusted look that conveyed that he understood the implications of what we were asking for better than we did. Here we were, two lost, borderline incoherent Phish concert attendees who might not have been entirely sober, begging to be let into the backseat of a cop car. So he could drive us to our hotel. We apparently lingered under the misconception that Miami police cars magically turned into free taxis at the stroke of midnight.

Neither of us saw anything unusual or counterproductive about trying desperately to get into a cop car. Part of that was attributable to the MDMA; we were not quite in our right minds. But there was also some strange lizard part of my brain that assumed that since I was a middle-class white man who paid his taxes on time and maintained an excellent credit rating (or did at the time), the police worked for me. As a rage-choked teenager growing up in a group home for emotionally disturbed adolescents, the police were the enemy. I hated cops and rich people. As an adult, I now apparently felt the police force were my employees. I had become the enemy. After thirty-three years I finally began to experience the transgressive surge of power that comes with white male privilege.

In Miami there seemed to be an implicit pact between the city and Phish fans. As long as no one got hurt, the city would turn a blind eye to a wide array of misdemeanors and misbehavior: public drunkenness, pot smoking, scalping, acid, mush-rooms, giggling men-children lying dazed on the ground next to deflated balloons, the whole doped-up shebang. They might not have liked the invasion of overgrown adolescents that descended upon their city, but they tolerated us because we pumped cash into the local economy. Besides, the whole city was built on coke money from the eighties, so who were they to look down on us for smoking some weed, huffing nitrous, or rolling on E?

After trying and failing to score a ride home with a cop, we finally managed to flag down a black cabdriver who seemed ter-rified of the erratic strangers racing into the middle of the street to stop his cab. "What the hell are you doing out here! You could get killed in this neighborhood at this time of night!" he yelled at us en route to our hotel. We paid him no never mind, for we'd been saved! We'd lived to rock another day. We fell asleep that night secure in the knowledge that we'd cheated death and that the grand finale of our great adventure lay just around the corner. Phish! Miami! New Year's Eve! Woo! Hoo! USA! USA!

EXPLODING INTO THE
TURBULENT TEENS:
PHISH, NEW YEAR'S EVE,
MIAMI

On New Year's Eve, Cadence and I still hadn't secured tickets to that night's show. At our hotel that afternoon we rode in an elevator with a red-haired kid wearing sunglasses and the official jam-band uniform of shorts, a T-shirt, and sandals. At the risk of seeming unhippified, my first impression was, "Jesus, look at that fucking burnout. What a waste."

Sure enough, when we got off the elevator he began to babble about his hunt for tabs of acid.

"You can probably get that at the Lot," Cadence offered cheerfully.

"Nah, man. I know a guy. It's all set up."

Of course you do, I thought cynically. "We're probably headed over to the Lot ourselves later to see if we can get tickets for tonight's show," Cadence continued.

"You guys need tickets? 'Cause I totally have some I could sell you at face value," the crimson-haired burnout offered. We accepted.

After we bought the tickets, Cadence asked the kid if he was a native of Miami. "Nah," he explained, "I'm just treating myself 'cause I just finished medical school."

"Where?" Cadence asked.

"Uh, Brown?"

It was a beautiful moment. Here were two proud products of Ivy League graduate schools who would one day look after your children and perform your open-heart surgery. But on December 31, 2009, they were primarily concerned with getting fucked up for that night's Phish show.

"This is just how I get my rocks off," he offered by way of explanation, half apologetically, half proudly.

At the show that night everyone around us was immersed in their own private spiritual reverie. To our right, a swarthy young man with the brooding intensity of a beat poet inhaled from a joint, then thrust his arms high in the air as if lost in a trance. Next to him, a shirtless young gent with homemade glitter-coated angel wings danced. It felt ridiculous and foreign and strangely right.

Phish's rise, fall, and rebirth lent an added poignancy to their performance of "Joy," the title track from their comeback album. On the tenth anniversary of Big Cypress, Anastasio sang the song with a disarming vulnerability that did much to wash away the lingering odor of Coventry and the drug bust. He poured himself into the lyrics with a sincerity that bordered on the heroic. When Anastasio sang, "We want you to be happy because this is your song too," he was commenting powerfully on the intense relationship between the band and its fans; every Phish song belongs to the audience as much as the band.

McConnell's organ and piano took center stage on a pair of Rolling Stones covers from *Exile on Main Street* that luxuriated in ramshackle grace: "Shine a Light" and the set-closing "Loving Cup."

"There's such a different vibe than the last time they toured," reflected Cadence. But for me it was like catching the last ten minutes of a movie. I was intrigued by all that came before—the backstories, the breakups and addictions and incarcerations— but was more than a little lost. The chorus to "Simple," which they played during their second set, goes, "We've got it simple 'cause we're in a band." But there's nothing simple about being in a band. Throw in money and fame and adulation and the situation becomes deeply complicated.

Yet Anastasio and bassist Mike Gordon seemed to experience uncomplicated pleasure as they performed an entire song moving in unison while jumping on trampolines.

As the band's New Year's Eve gag, it was announced that Jon Fishman would be blasted out of a cannon high into the stadium's rafters. After much fanfare and a deafening boom, Fishman disappeared. Anastasio then asked if there was a drummer in the house who could fill in for their fallen comrade, at which point a "woman" who looked suspiciously like Fishman in a wig and dress volunteered and manned the drums for the rest of the show.

Anastasio sang the names of everyone who made the tour possible while the band played "Blue Moon" behind him, giving props to everyone from the lowliest roadie to the loftiest guitar tech. He impishly introduced the band's head of security, for example, as the man who would be confiscating the crowd's nitrous tanks immediately after the show. It was all very geeky, very silly, and very sweet.

There was a celebratory quality to the show, and not just because it was New Year's Eve. The crowd was celebrating Anastasio's return from the abyss. They were celebrating Phish's resurrection from the dead. They were celebrating themselves and their bond with the band and the ghosts of a thousand past shows. They were celebrating four men who created something much bigger than themselves when they got together to perform music. They were celebrating being alive. I was celebrating being alive. I was celebrating being in love.

The crowd seemed to be moving as one, to have evolved into an orgiastic hive mind, grooving and grinding deliriously to a borderline transcendent performance. Phish and their fans had to wade through an awful lot of darkness to get to the light. The exuberance was hard-won.

At midnight balloons rained down from the rafters and I kissed Cadence. There was nowhere in the world I would rather be at that moment than in Miami, with Cadence, on New Year's Eve, watching Phish. I was living in the sacred present tense.

I was exhilarated by the journey that lay ahead of me, a voyage through strange corners of the pop music world where saner souls feared to tread. I wanted to lose and find myself in these alien worlds. I would become the world's least likely chameleon.

My time in Miami had come to an end but my adventure, or rather our adventure, had only just begun. Had I known what lay ahead of that delirious moment in Miami, I would have been filled with equal parts dread and anticipation, but in that moment all I felt was pure, rapturous joy.

AND NOW FOR SOMETHING COMPLETELY DIFFERENT: VIOLENT J'S *BEHIND THE PAINT* USHERS US INTO THE WORLD OF THE DARK CARNIVAL

Given the centrality of circus iconography in Insane Clown Posse's mythology, it might make sense to think of me as a ringmaster presiding over a three-ring circus perpetually threatening to spin out of control. In one ring lies the festival of light that is a Phish tour. In the next, intrepid adventurers will discover the Dark Carnival of Insane Clown Posse, while in the final ring, unbeknownst to me at the beginning of my bizarre ride, lie my rapidly degenerating psyche and crumbling sense of self.

So as your unreliable tour guide, I would like to warn you of a rather jarring shift in focus just ahead as we turn our attention from my introduction to Phish to my descent into the heart of the Dark Carnival at the 2010 Gathering of the Juggalos. But before we travel to Juggalo country, let's go straight to the source and learn about the secret history of Insane Clown Posse and the strange world it created from face paint, imagination, and stubborn persistence from Violent J's massive 2003 memoir *Behind the Paint.*

Violent J embodies a bifurcated identity as both an ostracized ninth-grade dropout *and* as a spiritual leader whose prophetic visions show the way to the eternal paradise of Shangri-La. Violent J is a man completely devoid of pretensions beyond his stubborn contention that he is a portal to a vast and unknowable spiritual realm beyond our comprehension. He's a regular dude, but he's also, you know, a makeshift prophet.

J writes of his discovery of the Dark Carnival and the Joker's Cards, the key components of the Insane Clown Posse mythology, "Now let me ask you, do you think I'm smart enough to come up with something like that on my own? I am a fucking dumb-ass; I never got past eighth grade, remember? Now, however, I've shown hundreds of thousands of people the same magic. And they feel it too. Juggalos are everywhere! Can't you see that it's magic? Look at how lame I am. Look how untalented we are, yet we have hundreds of thousands who follow the magic? Why? Cause it's real. Cause it IS magic."

Behind the Paint is a book equally defined by sputtering rage at a world that won't accept him no matter how successful he becomes and seemingly incongruous but pervasive sentimentality.

For example, when Violent J was four years old his older brother, Rob, caught a giant, magnificent butterfly. They were overjoyed. They were poor kids with nothing but each other and vivid imaginations, so something as seemingly inconsequential as catching a butterfly carried tremendous symbolic significance, but not nearly as much as there'd be after what happened next.

J and Rob made a home for the butterfly, but when they woke up the next morning to release their guest for the night they discovered the butterfly had died. For J, it was the childhood equivalent of Adam noshing on a McIntosh; the end of the innocence, the fall from grace.

Rob and his brother made a makeshift casket for the butterfly out of a potato chip can and buried their fallen comrade while reciting the following vow: "One day, we will make it to heaven, so that we can make sure the Butterfly made it, and so that we can apologize to that Butterfly face-to-face (If insects are not allowed in heaven, then we would ask to change that policy on the Butterfly's behalf.)"

Violent J got a giant tattoo on the inside of his left arm in honor of the Butterfly and dedicates every major accomplishment in his life to the Butterfly, including *Behind the Paint*. When contemplating ICP's complicated legacy, it's important to bear in mind the image of a four-year-old latchkey kid weeping uncontrollably alongside his six-year-old brother while burying a butterfly that symbolized all that was good and beautiful and pure in the world.

Behind the Paint offers an origin story for Insane Clown Posse, Violent J, and the Dark Carnival that marries the mundane with the fantastic. In a section helpfully titled MAJOR CHILDHOOD MEMORY 2, J writes of his mother traveling to Boston with a wealthy family to look after their children. This was a big deal for a five-year-old and a seven-year-old whose mother never left Michigan, but it was nothing compared to the windfall J's mom left behind for food: fifty dollars. Of course it's not advisable to leave prepubescent children alone, but J's broken home was desperately poor, and though J loves his mother dearly and thinks of her and his older brother as the heroes of his childhood, circumstances and finances forced her to make difficult concessions, like leaving her children at home while she struggled to make ends meet.

This fortune attracted the attentions of a ten-year-old bully who decided to crash over at J's home in a bid to get his hands on all the chips and dip, pizza, and sparkler J purchased with his mother's money.

J and his brother were appropriately terrified until they were visited in the middle of the night by what J describes as a black oil figure as dark as midnight that climbed up the stairs leading to J's room, raised and then lowered its hand, then floated downstairs and disappeared as mysteriously as it arrived. The sight of this mysterious creature inspired rapturous joy and much frantic screaming from J and Rob, but the neighborhood bully didn't see a thing.

This cryptic creature was, in J's own words, "GOD! No question, no doubt in my mind. It was God. Fuck you if you don't believe me. We know what we saw that night. G-O-D diggity himself. The Holy Roller Thunder Bowler, funky fresh in the flesh. GOD baby."

To J, God appeared to him and his brother one magical evening to let them know that everything was going to be all right and they had nothing to fear, not even malevolent prepubescent monsters intent on relieving them of their tasty snacks. What poor kid doesn't need that reassurance, supernatural or otherwise?

More than most poor children, J needed something to believe in. *Behind the Paint* is ingratiatingly devoid of subtext; J acknowledges the role daydreaming played in his survival when he writes of his brother and himself, "Fantasy kept us happy and busy. Rob and I were out on our own; from the time I was nine I was mentally gone. I stayed in a fantasyland and I'M STILL THERE."

Violent J's genius lies in roping an entire world of troubled, bored, angry, and confused kids into his elaborate fantasy world, in constructing a mythology and a worldview irresistible to outsiders and misfits.

As a kid, Violent J envied his older brother Rob's deep involvement in role-playing games like Dungeons & Dragons. J wanted to join in, but he could never figure out the complex rules. The Dark Carnival consequently became J's homemade version of Dungeons & Dragons, an elaborate mythology where J could map out the contours and details of his own epic creation.

Like his hero Michael Jackson, J created a hermetic universe where childhood never has to end. The Gathering of the Juggalos offers fans a purposeful regression back to the simple pleasures of childhood. It's an invitation to a world where adults can frolic on a Moon Bounce, enjoy the magic of fire at Hog Daddy's Hell Pit, take a helicopter ride, chow down on a hot dog at Violent J's Big Barbecue Bash or watch, in acid-stoked wonder, stilt walkers. It's a world of clowns and wrestlers and magicians full of role-playing and exhibitionism and mindless self-indulgence. The attendees of the Gathering are essentially children. Horny, drug-addled, belligerent children with erections and access to a wide array of mood-altering substances. Perhaps that's why people are so afraid of them. And secretly envious.

School had nothing to offer a fatherless, seemingly direction-less man like Violent J. He dropped out of the ninth grade and found other outlets for his restlessness. He watched kung-fu movies and wrestled and had boyish misadventures with a buddy named Joseph Utsler, whom the world would come to know as Shaggy 2 Dope. In an early burst of inspiration, J joined Shaggy 2 Dope as the leaders of an undistinguished organization named Inner City Posse that was part makeshift gang and part make-shift gangsta rap group.

In what only appears to be a paradox, J is supremely nostalgic for a childhood that sucked. Or rather he's nostalgic for the ele-ments of his childhood that allowed him to forget, if only for a moment, how badly his life sucked: ninja movies on UHF, cheap soda pop, the friendship of his brother and later a motley aggre-gation of wrestling geeks, and, above all else, an imagination that would be his salvation.

In time, J's reality would exceed his wildest fantasies. The wrestling-addicted misfit and backyard wrestler would briefly fight alongside Shaggy 2 Dope in the World Wrestling Federation in 1998 at the height of its unlikely mainstream fame before establishing in 1999 his very own wrestling league, Juggalo Championship Wrestling, which continues to thrive to this day and is a major component of the group's legendary Gathering of the Juggalos festival.

The night J had a brainstorm and changed the name and image of his struggling young gangsta rap group from Inner City Posse to Insane Clown Posse, he experienced a terrifying vision of a clown. The clown spoke to J in a loud, sinister voice that J could not understand. Suddenly J found himself inside a Felliniesque carnival full of wonders and horrors: roller coasters that reached to the sky, a twenty-story house of mirrors. In J's words, this circus of terror was "twisted and strange as fuck."

The clown in his dream held an outsize deck of joker cards that he dropped on the ground one at a time. As the clown ran out of cards J was rocketed high into the air, where he could see the whole sprawling carnival and surrounding town. He woke up a new man with a divine purpose. Nothing would ever be the same again.

The name change from Inner City Posse to Insane Clown Posse brought with it a change of direction. The gangsta rap of Inner City Posse gave way to a horrorcore aesthetic similar to Detroit pioneer Esham, who would one day record for Insane Clown Posse's Psychopathic Records. In the waning days of Inner City Posse, Violent J noticed that a hype man painted up like a clown got an enthusiastic response from the audience. When Inner City Posse morphed into Insane Clown Posse, it was decided that the entire group—which then also included

Shaggy 2 Dope's brother John Kickjazz, who would leave Insane Clown Posse following the release of its debut, *Carnival of Carnage*—would perform painted up as wicked clowns.

In the days that followed J's epiphany, he came to understand that he had been put on earth to drop a series of "Joker's Cards" in the form of albums designed to purify listeners and prepare them for the afterlife by forcing them to confront the wickedness and iniquity within their own souls. The Joker's Cards function as a dark mirror that reveals hidden truths about whoever peers into them. Each Joker's Card represents a supernatural force with a moral message to impart.

The first Joker's Card arrived in the form of 1992's *Carnival of Carnage,* a concept album about class warfare at its most overt, about bringing the pain of the downtrodden to the living rooms of the oligarchs who oppress them. The second Joker's Card, 1994's *Ringmaster,* focused on the impresario of the Carnival of Carnage, a macabre figure created through sin who helps determine whether the dead will ascend to Shangri-La or descend to the bowels of Hell's Pit. *The Riddlebox,* from 1995, introduced Juggalos to the equally sinister figure of a mysterious jack-in-the-box adorned by a faded question mark that the dead encounter upon shedding their mortal coil.

In 1997 the fourth Joker's Card dropped in the form of *The Great Milenko,* an album about a ghoulish necromancer who tries to tempt humanity into indulging its worst instincts. That album was followed by *The Amazing Jeckel Brothers,* which centers on a pair of brothers, one good (Jake) and one bad (Jack), who juggle fireballs representing the sins of the dead.

The Dark Carnival mythology gave Insane Clown Posse's music, iconography, and ideology something rare and precious in low-budget trash culture: an intriguing element of mystery. Insane Clown Posse songs pointed to a greater whole the full meaning of which would not be revealed for years or even decades to come. For kids who grew up on wrestling and fast food and video games, Insane Clown Posse offered both the thrill of instant gratification and the tantalizing promise that there was always more to come. As J writes in *Behind the Paint,* "Other rap groups were putting out singles. We were releasing the end of the world on an installment fuckin' plan."

J expounded on the enigmatic appeal of the Dark Carnival mythology when he told me, during one of two interviews I conducted with him for the *A. V. Club,* "There's nothing to study about [other] bands. There's nothing to uncover. There are no secrets. It's just all about the latest single. They don't even respect each other. And the fans in the crowd are the same way. They don't even respect each other. Juggalos are a whole different story.

"There are secrets to uncover about the band. There's stuff to uncover, the fact that there's secrets and things, that keeps it exciting. They keep it about more than a fancy hook. For a collector, it goes on forever. There's stuff to collect and find, and rarities—forever. I just think there's a lot to being a Juggalo. There's a lot to keep you busy, uncovering these things, and traveling to special gatherings and special events, and carpooling with people you don't even know, but they're all Juggalo family, so it's okay."

Insane Clown Posse's story transcends hip-hop. It transcends music. In many ways, it transcends entertainment altogether. It's a story about alienation and family and loneliness and sadness and anxiety and imagination and ego and resentment and fame.

At a time when hip-hop nakedly embraced crass consumerism and unabashed materialism, Insane Clown Posse romanticized poverty and outsiderdom, albeit in its own grubby scrub fashion. In a culture obsessed with wealth, social standing, beauty, and competition, there's something liberating and transgressive about a group that tells kids with nothing that being poor is cooler than being rich and that being a loser, a scrub, and a Juggalo is infinitely better than being a winner. Jay-Z brags about drinking Cristal because he's rich and can afford it even if his fans can't; Violent J and Shaggy 2 Dope rap about bargain-priced Faygo soda because it's dirt-cheap and anyone can afford it. Violent J and Shaggy 2 Dope transform weaknesses into strengths. Insane Clown Posse can't do anything to help their fans scale the wall of upward mobility, but they've made them feel better about where they are.

Even in their early days, Insane Clown Posse never simply performed music. It wasn't about virtuoso displays of lyricism, witty freestyles, or devastating battle raps: It was about putting on a show. And if the show looked and felt more like a backyard wrestling match or haunted house or sideshow than a rap concert, the fans weren't complaining. On the contrary, the fans were ecstatic.

Violent J reasoned that if Insane Clown Posse always behaved like big shots, then the world would treat them accordingly. They were convinced that if they cracked the local market, then major labels would scoop them up.

It didn't quite work out that way. Insane Clown Posse did break wide open in Detroit. They weren't just a local act; they were a local phenomenon. During an early show, Violent J noticed a heckler flipping him off, so he unscrewed the cap from a two-liter of Faygo (the group kept a bucket onstage) and whipped it at him. A dead show suddenly became a riot of carbonated madness as Insane Clown Posse sprayed the crowd with soda. A bewildering new tradition was born. It might have seemed patently ridiculous to non-Juggalos, but it was another way to set ICP apart from artists who performed only music.

At another concert, Violent J started playing with the title of one of Insane Clown Posse's earliest songs, "The Juggla," and accidentally stumbled upon a word for his fans that would live in infamy: *Juggalo.*

Insane Clown Posse fans now had a distinct identity. They weren't just poor kids from shitty neighborhoods in Michigan who got drunk and high and indulged in curious rituals; they were Juggalos. They had a name. They had traditions. That gave them a form of power. Following Insane Clown Posse wasn't something they did. It was who they were. Even more than Phish followers, fandom defined them. It set them apart from the rest of the world and drew a thick, impregnable line between Insane Clown Posse fans and everyone else. The group didn't seem to have casual fans: Either you had a fucking Hatchetman neck tattoo, or you thought they were a crime against music. There was precious little in between.

Being a Juggalo entailed a level of commitment inconceivable to most. It wasn't enough to simply listen to the albums or go to the shows. No, Juggalos had to wear clown makeup and adopt new Juggalo personas and evangelize on the duo's behalf to uncomprehending, sometimes judgmental and scathingly critical friends. They had to buy the merchandise. They had to become walking billboards for Insane Clown Posse, Psychopathic Records, and its wildly successful, enduring apparel line, HatchetGear. Around the time *branding* became a nauseating buzzword, Insane Clown Posse were intuitive geniuses at it. They were gods of self-promotion, face-painted P. T. Barnums of hip-hop. Ringmasters.

Yet the duo's astonishing, almost unprecedented local success (the only other competition was Esham and a redneck dude who called himself Kid Rock) didn't lead to offers from major labels. Major labels didn't understand Insane Clown Posse or its fans.

Insane Clown Posse understood, on a profound level, how to reach poor, angry, directionless kids hungering for any form of escape from the drudgery of their everyday lives. The group knew how to get people emotionally invested in the Joker's Cards and Dark Carnival because they were so emotionally invested themselves.

J happily conceded as much when I asked him if he still considered himself a scrub and he answered, "In my heart and in my soul. We're scrubs, man. We're the underdogs, we're blue collar, we're not VIP. We're fucking fast food man, we're not caviar."

When Insane Clown Posse looked at their ecstatic audience they saw themselves. When major label executives looked at Insane Clown Posse's audience, they saw something much different.

Class played a huge role. All fan bases are not created equal.

As in every other aspect of American society, there is a class-based hierarchy of fans. At the very pinnacle lie Radiohead fans and NPR subscribers, wealthy, desirable, well-behaved bourgeois bohemians with impeccable taste and plenty of disposable income. At the very bottom lie Juggalos. The music industry did not value these people. Society didn't value them either. But Violent J and Shaggy 2 Dope did. They do. That must be extraordinarily validating. The world treats Juggalos like freaks, but they are always welcome in the literal big tent of the Dark Carnival.

Finally, Insane Clown Posse's local success became too big for even the most conservative major label executives to ignore. The prospect of scoring a big payday off a band with a rabid built-in fan base overrode their personal and professional contempt for the duo. Somebody was making a fuckload of money off the wicked clowns. It might as well be them.

So hip-hop, boy band, and R&B giant Jive held its nose, swallowed its pride, and signed Insane Clown Posse to a contract with a modest advance. Violent J imagined that Jive would use its corporate clout and muscle to break Insane Clown Posse nationally. If the rest of the country embraced Insane Clown Posse with the fervor and devotion of the duo's hometown, then there was no limit to the heights they could climb. The little horrorcore duo that could would finally be playing in the big leagues.

In *Behind the Paint*, Violent J has a vivid phrase that succinctly encapsulates the dramatic twist of fate that transformed Insane Clown Posse from put-upon poindexters to the world's least likely pop stars this side of the Benedictine Monks: scrubs fucking cheerleaders. For Violent J, it was a profoundly mixed blessing: He obviously enjoyed having sex with women who never would have given him the time of day in high school, but the hedonistic kicks were undercut by the understanding that these women were interested in him only as a celebrity, a pop star, a local hero. They all wanted to fuck a pop star named Violent J, not a fat, lonely, vulnerable outcast named Joseph Bruce.

This last point was tragicomically illustrated when Violent J invited a particularly hot groupie onto his tour bus. The groupie promised to rock his world the moment the tour bus reached the hotel, but when a member of Insane Clown Posse's entourage smacked the hot-to-trot young lady on the ass, she turned around and hissed, "You're not important enough to touch me." The groupie's actions were understandable—sleeping with Violent J does not give everyone associated with him license to smack her ass—but Violent J nevertheless had an epiphany and kicked the groupie off the bus. He learned the hard way that fucking the cheerleaders of the world didn't make him anything less of a scrub; it just made him a scrub rich and famous enough to appeal to women who derive their self-esteem from casual sex with famous people.

It turns out Jive didn't love Violent J or Insane Clown Posse any more than the aforementioned groupie. In signing Insane Clown Posse, they saw an opportunity to make a quick, dirty buck with a group already equipped to move albums and merchandise. Jive thought Insane Clown Posse was ugly as fuck, but hot damn if their selling power didn't make them beautiful.

But Jive showed no interest in exposing Insane Clown Posse

to a national audience. The last thing it wanted to do was broadcast to the world that it had gotten into bed with the reviled iconoclasts from Detroit. The duo remained an embarrassment to Jive and to the music industry at large—Jive simply hoped it was an embarrassment that could make money.

Violent J understandably nurses a persecution complex of Nixonian proportions, but even he didn't realize the full extent of his label's contempt for him, his fans, and his music. As the duo's stint as major-label musicians approached its final death throes, an executive at Jive hipped Insane Clown Posse to the real reason why its support was nonexistent: "I never told you this," confided the executive, "but some of the people at the label thought the 'Chicken Huntin'' song [the single] was racist toward black people. They thought the whole clown makeup thing was you guys making fun of black people rapping."

Violent J didn't don face paint and reinvent himself as a scary clown to push hyperaggressive hip-hop clichés past the point of absurdity. He donned face paint and reinvented himself as a scary clown because wrestling and his brother's role-playing hobby taught him the value of showmanship and surprise, of baiting audiences and having an immediately identifiable gimmick.

I doubt Violent J considered the troubling racial connotations of smearing on face paint and performing black music. I doubt he's familiar with the myriad permutations of minstrelsy, past and present. When he conceived of the Dark Carnival, or rather when the Dark Carnival revealed itself to him in the form of a prophetic vision, he wasn't in a *Bamboozled* state of mind. When he decided to put on the face paint for the first time he was a failed would-be gangsta rapper whose pre–Insane Clown Posse outfit, Inner City Posse, impressed no one with its street credibility or lyrical ability. He was looking for that tricky X factor that would catapult him from wannabe to star.

In the Dark Carnival, he found it. On a pragmatic level, Joseph Bruce will be the first to concede that he is not a particularly handsome man, and black-and-white clown paint transformed him from a guy who looks like he should be slicing ham at Subway to a larger-than-life figure of menace and fun. For Bruce at least, becoming a wicked clown constituted a big step up.

Yet people looked down on Insane Clown Posse and Juggalos. The perception conformed to narrow, reductive stereotypes about how poor, uneducated white people think and behave. The irony, of course, is that people who know nothing about ICP—yet very strongly believe that their music is worthless and their fans are illiterate and racist—are doing exactly what they accuse ICP of doing: forming concrete ideas about how an entire group of people think and act based on their appearance, place on the socioeconomic ladder, and the kind of music they enjoy. Only instead of deciding that all black kids who wear baggy jeans and listen to gangsta rap must be drug dealers, gang members, or high school dropouts, the ICP-is-racist contingent decided that poor white kids who rock ICP tattoos and listen to horrorcore must be racist. And also gang members and high school dropouts.

Insane Clown Posse makes music for Juggalos. It has always been ambivalent about crossing over into the mainstream, but when one of the major labels of the Disney Music Group, Hollywood Records, plunked down a cool $1 million to buy the duo's contract from Jive, it obviously had a lot more on its mind than making sure Violent J and Shaggy 2 Dope sell out the Fillmore in Detroit every Halloween for their annual Hallowicked concert.

Disney and ICP. It would be hard to imagine a stranger or less feasible union, but Hollywood nevertheless felt it could break the duo nationally in a way Jive never could. It was scrubs fucking cheerleaders all over again—or in this instance, scrubs fucking Mouseketeers. For a brief idyll it appeared that Insane Clown Posse might just become MTV fixtures and mainstream superstars after all.

While Insane Clown Posse lurched erratically toward the mainstream, MTV and pop radio fell hopelessly in love with Insane Clown Posse's two biggest local rivals. The mainstream made Violent J and Shaggy 2 Dope wait and wait and wait, only to give it up to Kid Rock and Eminem mere minutes into their first date.

Kid Rock would become a huge pop star, but the cultural supernova that is Eminem dwarfed him. Violent J first learned of Eminem's existence when the scrappy young rapper handed him a flyer to an upcoming record-release show promising guest appearances by Kid Rock and . . . Insane Clown Posse?

In an impressive act of chutzpah and dishonesty, Eminem semipromised an appearance by a popular local act without ever bothering to ask ICP if they'd perform. J was, to put it mildly, not amused.

This incident sparked a feud between Eminem and ICP that involved numerous dis songs, bad blood, and a notorious incident in which Eminem was arrested for pulling a gun on an ICP affiliate named Doug Dail. Rather than hype their feud with Eminem to sell books and generate controversy in the media, Violent J relegates his group's explosive conflict with the best-selling rapper of the past decade to a mere footnote.

That might seem a little perverse, considering Eminem's massive fame and the public's enduring fascination with him, but *Behind the Paint* is a book for Juggalos, and within the context of the Dark Carnival, Eminem is a minor figure at best. Insane Clown Posse is doomed to be a minor footnote in the Eminem saga. So Violent J returned the favor.

J strikes an unmistakably Nixonian figure. ICP's appeal to its fans echoes Nixon's plea to his Silent Majority. Both loudly proclaim to their disgruntled followers that the elites of the world don't like them, that they think they're stupid and worthless and beneath their contempt, but that they understand and empathize with them on a profound level because they are them. Nixon put no distance between himself and his followers. Nor does Violent J.

Eminem is JFK to Violent J's Nixon. He's the pretty boy with two of the most powerful people in music behind him: Interscope head Jimmy Iovine and producer Dr. Dre. *Behind the Paint* emphasizes the mundane legwork and incessant self-promotion behind Insane Clown Posse's success to an almost perverse degree.

Violent J and Shaggy 2 Dope's fortunes began to change when Disney recalled what was to be the duo's Hollywood debut, *The Great Milenko,* from stores mere hours after its release and canceled ICP's national tour and in-store appearances. In the

blinding light of Southern Baptist protests about Disney affiliate ABC airing *Ellen* and unofficial "Gay Days" at Disneyland,
Insane Clown Posse went from being a dirty little moneymaker
to a public humiliation piled on top of others. The Mouse, it
seems, was not as down with the clown as it originally let on.
ICP signed to Island.

Getting dropped by the Mouse proved to be a badge of countercultural authenticity; the ultimate embodiment of wholesome
American values was exorcising these clown-faced demons from
their holy body and casting them off into the wilderness.

After years of endless toil and diligently building a fan base,
Insane Clown Posse wanted a seat at the table. They wanted to
be recognized and respected for all they had accomplished, but
in a society and pop culture where money can buy just about
anything, Insane Clown Posse discovered that there were limits
to what their money, clout, and popularity could attain.

By 1999, Insane Clown Posse had gotten about as far as any
act can without scoring a radio hit or substantial play on MTV.
The group understandably wanted to change that, so a crack
unit of Juggalos and Psychopathic Records affiliates decided to
launch a strategic strike deep into the heart of enemy territory:
MTV's *Total Request Live*.

The infidels were at the gate. Insane Clown Posse's website
directed its fans to all totally request its music video "Let's Go
All the Way" on *Total Request Live* and show up at MTV's Times
Square Studio in a painted-up frenzy. The scrubs were shutting
down cheerleader practice and angrily demanding mass blow
jobs. Some four hundred Juggalos showed up in Times Square

toting homemade signs angrily demanding that MTV let Violent J and Shaggy 2 Dope be afforded the same exposure the network previously afforded such paragons of artistic integrity as Don Johnson, Milli Vanilli, and its very own Jesse Camp.

It was just like Martin Luther King's March on Washington, only completely different. The Psychopathic Records family had dubbed the strategic strike on the Lost Isle of Carson "The Mighty Day of Lienda," meaning "The Mighty Day of All or Nothing." At the end of the day, its sneak attack on Viacom's inner sanctum was either going to expose the duo to a vast new audience or Insane Clown Posse would be crushed by the jackbooted forces of cultural repression.

In pop culture terms it was Little Big Horn, and Violent J was General Custer: Hundreds of Juggalos were forcibly removed from Times Square, outside the MTV studios, by security, and the Insane Clown Posse video was deemed ineligible for *Total Request Live* since apparently MTV needs to okay videos before they're eligible for the show.

Violent J had transformed Insane Clown Posse into a cultural force, however maligned and controversial, by always listening to his inner carny, and his inner carny told him the stunt would make news whether or not it was successful. Hell, it'd probably make bigger news if MTV *didn't* bend to the will of the Juggalo masses and play the video.

As Insane Clown Posse and its fans welcomed in a new millennium and prepared for the first Gathering in 2000, Violent J was faced with a formidable challenge: What would the sixth, final, and definitive Joker's Card be? Considering the role the

Joker's Cards play within the mythology of the Dark Carnival, it was a question and a conundrum of the utmost importance.

Nobody ever said being a prophet was easy. As the time neared to reveal the final, climactic Joker's Card, Violent J began to buckle under the stress. During a concert in April of 1998 he experienced a panic attack, blacked out, and cut off his signature dreadlocks. By his own admission, Violent J was fat, depressed, and out of shape.

Then two seminal events occurred that changed his life forever. In *Behind the Paint,* J writes passionately about lolling about in a depressed haze one night, lazily masticating on his favored dish of sour cream with noodles, and literally took a long, hard look in the mirror and was disgusted by what he saw: big black bags under his sunken eyes, long, matted, multicolored hair, and a big fat gut.

In a fit of self-loathing, Violent J decided he had to go somewhere, anywhere. Then something miraculous happened: J discovered walking. I'm not talking about the hardcore walking people do in specially designed outfits festooned with Nike swooshes in malls; I'm talking about plain old one-foot-in-front-of-the-other walking. J soon discovered that he loved to walk athletically; it set him free and released him from his demons.

The simplest thing in the world saved J. There's something incredibly poignant about that. Violent J really does have a childlike faith in the simplest of pleasures: a good bowl of sour-cream-and-noodle soup washed down with Faygo and a joint, followed by a brisk after-dinner walk. "I could write a whole book about my walking adventures," J writes with guileless enthusiasm in *Behind the Paint.* He has thus far chosen not to.

It wasn't Scientology or primal scream therapy that saved J: It was simple, easy, free walking. Walking gave him the time and the space needed to contemplate the most important task of his young life: revealing the final Joker's Card. The sixth Joker's Card would reveal Insane Clown Posse's ultimate message for the world. Would it be positive or negative? Would it be a revolutionary cry to overthrow a corrupt system, or a retreat into a hermetic world he could control? Would J go all L. Ron Hubbard on us and use the sixth Joker's Card as the foundation for a cult? Weren't Juggalos already something of a benign cult?

Finally, the identity of the sixth Joker's Card came to J: It would be the Wraith, or death itself. This was no ordinary Joker's Card. For starters, it came in two parts: The first was 2002's *The Wraith: Shangri-La,* while the second was 2004's *The Wraith: Hell's Pit.* The moral of the final, climactic Joker's Card was clear: Followers were to lead a moral existence and purge themselves of their sins and wickedness so that they might ascend to the eternal paradise of Shangri-La, or else they would descend for posterity into the waking nightmare of Hell's Pit.

The message of the Dark Carnival is ultimately moralistic and conventional: Live a good, virtuous life and receive the ultimate reward, or sin and roast in the bowels of hell. In the end, the message of the Dark Carnival wasn't too different from the morals imparted in Sunday school. To some Juggalos, that must have felt awfully anticlimactic. After those years of buildup and anticipation, they expected something more than a Juggalo reiteration of conventional morality.

The first deck of Joker's Cards ended as it must. For J ultimately isn't a cult leader or a religious philosopher: He's a dungeon master who came up with a cool game that got bigger and bigger and bigger until he couldn't figure out how to end it without sending everyone home vaguely disappointed and underwhelmed.

Insane Clown Posse had achieved just about everything but what it longed for most: the respect of its peers and the mainstream. After they left Island, ICP's days as major-label artists were over. Their days as Gold and Platinum artists were over. After the revelation of the sixth Joker's Card, Violent J's days as a homemade prophet were over, at least for the time being.

ICP IN A POST–JOKER'S CARD WORLD

Following the revelation of the final Joker's Card, the duo was forced to reexamine the direction of its career. If MTV had violently rejected Insane Clown Posse and critics continued to sneer, Insane Clown Posse discovered that the mainstream still had a number of roles for them to play, none of them flattering. The duo was still the default choice for worst-band-in-the-world honors.

My 2009 memoir contains snide references to both Phish and Insane Clown Posse. I wrote those sentences without bothering to actually listen to any of the music or go to any of their shows. Why would I? That might entail opening my mind to music and ways of life my judgmental peers and an often-sneering critical community had thoughtfully rejected for me out of hand.

When I met my half brother for the first time—we didn't meet until I was twenty-three—he took me to the mall to buy Insane Clown Posse merchandise and apparel from the Hatchet-Gear collection. He was an ex-con, a teenage father, and the son of a heroin-addicted bipolar Vietnam veteran whose testimony against my mother in divorce court helped my father win custody of my older sister and me. I joked in my memoir *The Big Rewind* that my half sibling being Down with the Clown provided conclusive evidence that nurture, or rather lack thereof, played a more crucial role in the emotional development of a child than nature.

My sibling fit the psychological profile of a Juggalo. He was raised by a mentally ill, pathologically self-absorbed mother in the heart of the St. Louis ghetto. Like so many Juggalos, he grew up in a home that wasn't just broken: It was shattered. Violently. He was born to a mother who had a baby by a profoundly broken man even after he had testified against her in court. I saw my brother's affection for Insane Clown Posse as incontrovertible proof of how fundamentally different we were.

Today, I think about it differently. I imagine a world in which my mother had gotten custody of me. I might have grown up to be a Juggalo myself. The kinship of fellow Juggalos might have filled the hole in my life left by parental abandonment.

In another lifetime, the ham-fisted parables of the Dark Carnival and the Joker's Cards might have excited my intellectual curiosity and led me on a vastly different path. Like all teenagers, I was a follower, a cultist in need of strong leaders to tell me what to do and listen to and read and how to lead my life. Only I swore allegiance to the gods of my particular tribe. I saw the films the more respectable, highbrow likes of Pauline Kael and Roger Ebert and the *Cahiers du Cinéma* gang told me to see and listened to the critically sanctioned Rebel Music favored by the Greil Marcuses of the world and read the books every young burgeoning intellectual is required to read lest he look foolish or unrefined in the eyes of fetching young coeds he hopes to impress/bed.

As the son of a University of Chicago graduate, I might not have fit the psychological profile of the Juggalo as neatly as my half brother, but I too came from a broken home and grew up feeling alienated and alone, ostracized and filled with rage. The difference, I suppose, comes down to expectations and taste. No matter how bad things got, it was always assumed I would go to college like my father before me and contribute something to society. The same could not be said of my half brother; college wasn't part of the universe he grew up in. I didn't have much growing up, but I clung to the notion that I had taste, refinement, and standards. The erudite critics who shaped how I saw the world had given me the life-affirming gift of being able to differentiate between art and schlock.

So Insane Clown Posse became a pop-culture punching bag for the cynical, smart-ass likes of me. They were a joke that had gone on for far too long, the mainstream had decided, and it was time to put an end to it once and for all.

As one of the founders of the Parents Music Resource Center, a committee formed in 1985 to warn parents of the dangers of potty mouths like Prince (whose risqué song "Darling Nikki," with its line about masturbating in a hotel lobby with a magazine, helped inspire the group's creation), Tipper Gore made a name for herself peddling a variation on the timeworn notion that rock and pop music and various metal and rap groups are a menace to society. Gore and the PMRC set out to have warning labels placed on albums with obscene content. The group succeeded in getting warning stickers on albums like ICP's *The Great Milenko,* but that didn't really leave it anywhere else to go.

Just when it appeared that the Music Menace Brigade had breathed its last overheated, hysterical breath, it roared back to life to alert mainstream America of a threat to its children greater than any since the fall of the Third Reich: Insane Clown Posse.

The renewed movement was spearheaded by a pair of clowns named Bill O'Reilly and Martin Bashir. O'Reilly's 2001 piece on Insane Clown Posse is pure Music Menace 101. In classic form, it begins by presenting Insane Clown Posse as demonic pied pipers that fly under the radar of most adults but are universally known, if not necessarily beloved, by their kids, before teasing a "stunning" interview just after the break.

Just before the interview, O'Reilly plays shamelessly to his overwhelmingly white, conservative middle-class audience's prejudices by quipping, "What [Insane Clown Posse] advocates makes some of the black rappers look like Shirley Temple." O'Reilly and his producers wanted to scare his audience, so they conjured up the most terrifying, threatening image they could imagine—black rappers—before announcing that there's something somehow *even worse*!

It doesn't matter if it's Elvis or the Rolling Stones or Jimi Hendrix or the Sex Pistols or Guns N' Roses or Snoop Dogg, the hysteria stays consistent: These swaggering badasses are going to corrupt our precious sons and daughters with their devil music, and quite possibly take their virginity while they're at it. And more often than not, they're going to do it with black music, whether they're black themselves or merely schooled in black musical traditions. It's altogether fitting that O'Reilly interviewed ICP as part of an ongoing series sanctimoniously titled "Children at Risk in America."

Violent J wasn't particularly familiar with O'Reilly before the interview, so he mounted his default defense: He's an entertainer, not a role model. J argued that it's ultimately up to parents to raise children and teach them morals, not clown-themed horrorcore rap duos.

There are few things in the world more alarming than clowns in nonclown contexts. Take a clown out of his natural habitat in circuses, sideshows, children's parties, and nightmares, and he becomes a walking punch line. Accordingly, it's utterly surreal to watch an ostensible newsman in a blue oxford shirt sit opposite a pair of men in clown makeup and treat them as a legitimate news story.

Violent J handles O'Reilly's badgering with the nervous defensiveness of an eighth grader being dressed down in front of the entire class; to Violent J, O'Reilly is just the latest in a long line of stuffy authority figures delivering stern lectures on the proper way to behave.

O'Reilly then springs what he apparently imagines is gotcha footage conclusively showing ICP in the act of corrupting young minds. As evidence for the prosecution in the case of *O'Reilly vs. ICP,* O'Reilly offers a brief exchange at an in-store signing where Violent J asked a twelve-year-old boy, "Did your nuts drop yet?"

This much is incontestable: As part of its ongoing commitment to stamping out injustice and elucidating profound truths, Fox News sent a crew out to an ICP in-store signing to clearly document Violent J asking the question "Did your nuts drop yet?" O'Reilly can't bring himself to utter such vile words, so, with palpable disgust in his voice and his body shivering with righteous indignation, O'Reilly paraphrases J as asking, "Did you drop your testicles yet?"

As Violent J answers O'Reilly's idiotic questions, a distinct reversal occurs: The seemingly sane man in a blue dress shirt begins to look like a frothing, hysterical moron, and the men in clown makeup become the voice of reason and restraint by default.

O'Reilly is only warming up. As his next gotcha clip, O'Reilly shows Violent J, apparently acting in his unofficial role as the universe's guidance counselor, asking a fourteen-year-old if he used drugs, then urging him to go home and "smoke something."

Violent J defends his actions as the kind of goofy ribbing a salty uncle might give a favorite niece or nephew.

"What if that kid goes home and smokes crack?" O'Reilly continues. Do you have any responsibility for it because you said it to him one-on-one?" To O'Reilly, Insane Clown Posse weren't just making music the elite disdained; now they were getting little Timmy hooked on crack cocaine as well. Are there any limits to their capacity for evil?

His voice quaking with anger, O'Reilly impatiently holds Insane Clown Posse responsible for being negligent father figures to an entire generation of lost youth when he urgently inquires, "How are they going to make it in the world, how are they going to have good relationships, to get a good job, support themselves, and raise families? How are they going to make it if they don't have any parents who care about them and they look up to you two and you two are telling them to smoke dope, to do sex stuff, to go out and get arrested and commit crimes, how are they going to possibly prosper with role models like you?"

To give O'Reilly credit, he *was* directly referencing the early ICP album *Smoke Dope and Do Sex Stuff* as well as their later EP *Go Out and Get Arrested and Commit Crimes* (they *do* have some awfully heavy-handed album titles). He's much better-versed in the duo's oeuvre than I had expected. To O'Reilly, ICP are more than just the worst role models imaginable. They're also monsters personally responsible for ensuring that their fans never have good relationships, get good jobs, support themselves, or raise families. That's an awful lot of responsibility to lay on anyone.

In the nine years separating O'Reilly's legendary 2001 summit with the clown-painted corrupters of youth and a 2010 profile on *Nightline,* the ICP menace only grew in strength and pure evil.

At least that's what Martin Bashir's March 9 exploration of the shadowy world of the Dark Carnival suggests. Bashir begins with lofty talk of "real-life murder and mayhem some believe may be motivated by a certain sound and stagecraft" before introducing Insane Clown Posse as a pair that "raps about acts of savagery and violence" while "some of their fans are living them" before asking, "Should the artists share in the blame?"

Like much of the mainstream media, Bashir exhibits a distinct tone-deafness when it comes to Insane Clown Posse. He seems intent on deliberately misunderstanding the duo, its fans, and its mythology in ways that support a preconceived thesis.

On *Nightline,* that thesis was, of course, that the Insane Clown Posse were poisoning the minds of their fans with sinister voodoo and transforming them into an army of miscreant mass murderers.

Bashir's talk of a "sound" that motivates "real-life acts of murder and mayhem" hearkens back to criticism that early rock 'n' roll's infernal jungle rhythms would transform the younger generation into a giant interracial bisexual fuckfest, and later hysteria that heavy metal bands somehow crafted subliminal messages that could only be heard when their records were played backwards. To the Music Menace folks, these albums and artists aren't just dangerous because of their lyrical content; the danger lies in the grooves themselves, in the power of noise to hypnotize and control. Endemic to this way of thinking is a pronounced lack of respect for the autonomy and intelligence of teenagers.

Bashir's piece adds a whole new wrinkle to the Music Menace

spiel: These agents of pure evil weren't just leading little Timmy astray. They're also the literal leaders of a vicious gang.

Nightline lays out its case in screaming tabloid hyperbole, flashing graphics like "JUGGALO" INSANITY over grim black-and-white footage of shaggy-haired Juggalo murderers being led away in handcuffs for their crimes. The venerable late-night news institution cynically tries to massage a pair of murders committed by self-identified Juggalos into a nationwide epidemic of horror-core-induced ultraviolence.

What the Juggalo murder squadron lacks in numbers it apparently makes up for in brutality. Not even Juggalos are safe from blood-crazed Juggalos. Bashir reports ominously of a twenty-one-year-old named Tony Lacasio who "called himself a Juggalo but it's alleged he snitched and lost his life." *Nightline* once represented the unassailable apogee of late-night journalistic excellence. Then it succumbed to the tabloid mania sweeping our culture and became a forum for reporting on "snitching" within the Juggalo community.

"We've got multiple individuals committing gang-related crimes, gang-motivated crimes, and they're using the name *Juggalo*," reports an Arizona cop in a dizzying torrent of frightening-sounding phrases that are vague to the point of meaninglessness. Who are these "multiple individuals"? Are there hundreds of thousands of them conspiring to overthrow the government? Or two dudes on meth in a trailer somewhere huffing paint thinner and listening to a CD of *The Great Milenko* on repeat? Doesn't "multiple" just mean there's more than one of them?

What exactly is a gang-related crime? How does it differ from a gang-motivated crime? And what does it mean to say that this fuzzy aggregation of gang-related, gang-motivated individuals is "using the name *Juggalo*"? These are all relevant queries the show has no interest in answering. Instead it lets a flurry of quick cuts of dead-eyed Juggalos being led away in handcuffs married to horror-movie music create the impression that Juggalos are everywhere and intent on murdering you and your family.

At the Gathering of the Juggalos, I found the constant chants of "Family! Family!" to be the strangely poignant cries of exiles from broken homes creating makeshift families to make up for backgrounds riddled with deadbeat dads and moms zonked out on pills and cheap booze. But within the context of the *Nightline* piece, footage of Juggalos guilelessly shouting "Family!" in unison takes on a sinister connotation. The "family" the piece means to invoke is less the brotherhood of man than a crime family, or the Manson family.

Bashir calls Insane Clown Posse "one of the most successful bands you've never heard of." Like O'Reilly, Bashir assumes that his audience knows nothing about Insane Clown Posse and consequently is liable to believe the worst about them, especially if it's presented in a quasi-news format by a man in a suit with an authoritative British accent. Bashir warns us that horrorcore videos are "all over YouTube" (not unlike similarly corrosive clips of cats flushing toilets). Then he takes us to the set of one of these promotional clips of the damned—a song that, in Bashir's weird turn of phrase, "characterizes murder"—called "In Your Face."

In what could very well represent a nadir in the history of journalism, if not civilization as a whole, Bashir sits down opposite Violent J and Shaggy 2 Dope and inquires solemnly, "How do you write a line like 'From Pluto to Uranus [pronounced crisply and clearly as *your anus*] we are underground famous'?"

What does that question even mean? Is Bashir legitimately interested in Insane Clown Posse's creative process? Does he want to know whether they favor internal rhyme schemes, alliteration, elaborate metaphors, or even iambic pentameter? Or is he inquiring whether Shaggy 2 Dope and Violent J memorize their lines rather than writing them down, à la Jay-Z and Eminem? Do they freestyle? Do they jot down rhymes in notebooks? How do they feel about thesauruses and rhyming dictionaries? Do they prefer complicated, polysyllabic Pharoahe Monch–style rhyme schemes or blunter, more forceful lyrical styles? Or is he just singling out a particularly juvenile lyric in an utterly redundant attempt to make a pair of middle-aged men in clown makeup look silly?

When Violent J tries to defend the lyrics as fresh, Bashir testily counters, "But isn't this almost prepubescent, barely literate writing?"

Once again, the fat man in the clown makeup pushing forty emerges as more civil, reasonable, and rational than the ostensible newsman alerting audiences to the Juggalo menace. With cheerful good humor, Violent J responds, "Probably to you, because you sound smart as a motherfucker."

GOOD-BYE, WOODSTOCK, HELLO, GATHERING OF THE JUGGALOS: CURIOUS TIMES IN CAVE-IN-ROCK

Insane Clown Posse's strange flirtation with the mainstream peaked with its appearance at Woodstock 99. The duo's appearance was considered controversial by fans who worried that these preeminent outsiders had sold out by appearing on the same bill as Sheryl Crow, Bruce Hornsby, and their old rival

Kid Rock. To J, Insane Clown Posse didn't pander to the mainstream by playing Woodstock 99; the mainstream pandered to Insane Clown Posse. J writes in his autobiography that Woodstock 99 paid the duo a cool hundred grand for a single set and afforded it complete creative freedom to go as Faygo crazy and carny theatrical as it pleased, boasting, "[Woodstock] sold out the mainstream style for us! Woodstock never came to us and asked us to change one fuckin' thing about us or our show! They wanted ICP just as ICP is, and nothing else. If that ain't fresh, then I don't know what the fuck is!"

As fresh as it might have been to play Woodstock 99, the infamous festival was most assuredly not Insane Clown Posse's party. They were the sideshow, not the main attraction.

That would not be the case at the very first Gathering of the Juggalos, an Insane Clown Posse–curated festival of arts and culture J's brother Rob (alternately known as rapper-wrestler Jumpsteady) put together that debuted in 2000 at Novi, Michigan's, Novi Expo Center.

An army of some seven thousand Juggalos descended upon the Novi Expo Center for the first Gathering, surprising even Insane Clown Posse with their sheer volume and dedication. The first Gathering was barely restrained chaos that eventually gave way to complete, unrestrained anarchy when Juggalos rushed the stage during Insane Clown Posse's climactic performance. The powers that be shut the show down before the frenzy escalated into a full-blown riot.

From the start, that was part of the appeal of Gathering of the Juggalos: It was a place where anything could happen and a riot was perpetually on the verge of breaking out. Novi, Michigan, did not want these curious young men and their even more curious fans to return to wreak more havoc, so the second Gathering took place at Seagate Center in Toledo, Ohio, where chaos once again erupted during the climactic performance and, according to an oral history on the festival in *Spin* by Christopher Weingarten (whom I would have the pleasure of hanging out with during my second Gathering), Violent J ended up beating a fan bloody with his microphone after he attempted to snatch Violent J's Hatchetman chain. To the surprise of no one, Insane Clown Posse was informed that it was no longer welcome in Toledo, and the festival migrated once again, this time to Peoria, Illinois, a small town well known for the cliché "Will it play in Peoria?" and desperate enough for revenue to welcome a group and its fans whose terrible reputation for vandalism and destruction essentially got them blacklisted from the nation's convention centers.

The third Gathering only contributed to the burgeoning countercultural institution's notoriety when Bubba Sparxxx was booed offstage and a riot broke out over an issue of central importance to Insane Clown Posse and its fans: naked breasts. When the police grabbed a woman flashing her breasts and her boyfriend, the crowd rebelled and tear gas was employed to break up the chaos.

Insane Clown Posse needed to find a nirvana where fans could expose their naked breasts and destroy things free from the prying eyes of those who do not understand. They seemingly found just that in Nelson Ledges Quarry Park in Portage County, Ohio, the sight of the fourth, fifth, and sixth Gatherings. In the woods of Ohio they found the freedom they'd been looking for, but even Portage County, Ohio, has a breaking point, and after the sixth Gathering the group was once again informed it would need to relocate its festival. After a muddy year in Pataskala, Ohio, the Gathering of the Juggalos found a seemingly permanent home in 2007 in a strange backwater town called Cave-in-Rock, Illinois, that I would come to develop a deep fondness for.

And it is in Cave-in-Rock, Illinois, at the tenth annual Gathering of the Juggalos, that my story and Insane Clown Posse's begin to overlap. Driving to Cave-in-Rock, I experienced the feeling of leaving civilization in search of a stark, beautiful, and savage new world. Cadence and I drove for miles without running across even the faintest reminder of human habitation. Long stretches of road boasted no illumination. We passed a prison. Cadence was alarmed until I assured her that should a prisoner ever escape, the many serial killers in the region would take him down before he could hurt anybody.

Cave-in-Rock is a place where hope goes to die, a grubby realm of clapboard churches and failing businesses in rust-covered converted trailers where a Ponderosa Steakhouse stands out as an oasis of civilization in a sea of small-town hopelessness. It was, in other words, prime Juggalo country.

I would come to identify with Juggalos in ways that troubled my friends and family, but I was still on the outside looking in when Cadence and I checked in at a Comfort Inn on August 15, 2010, where our call for a car service was answered by a dapper man in his midfifties who spoke in the booming, stentorian cadences of a professional speaker.

"You've a great voice," I said from the backseat. "Did you ever do any announcing or anything?"

"Why, yes," he answered, clearly pleased to be asked. "I used to do a fair amount of racetrack announcing back in the day." In fact, he seemed to have done a little bit of everything.

Like many of the townies, he was fascinated by the strange influx of clown-painted outsiders who pumped money and drugs into the infrastructure every year, then disappeared.

"Does this band, this clown band. Do they make a lot of money?" the driver asked fairly deep into a conversation that got more interesting and unexpected by the minute. The gentleman told us he had moved into the area because a Google search revealed that it had the highest concentration of people with postgraduate degrees in the country, but that other than membership in a nearby book club, he was woefully disappointed by Cave-in-Rock.

"Yeah. They do. They've never attained the breakout mainstream success of someone like Kid Rock or Eminem, but they've managed to hold on to substantive popularity for two decades in an incredibly hostile market, which is an incredible achievement," I answered.

He spied an opening. "I see." The man had a hypnotic habit of pausing dramatically before he said anything, almost as if waiting for words to appear on a teleprompter so he could deliver them as crisply and professionally as possible. "Of course the only time *I* ever cracked six figures or more in a year was when I liquidated my DeLorean dealership."

"Oh my God. You had a DeLorean dealership? What was

that like? What was *he* like?" I inquired excitedly, delighted to be in the presence of someone who knew eccentric and disgraced would-be automotive pioneer John DeLorean.

"He was," the driver paused dramatically again, "a complicated man. Very charismatic, but also very dark. He had the kind of magnetism that made you want to follow him, though we all know how that ended," he said just before he dropped us off at the Gathering.

It was well over a hundred degrees when Cadence and I entered the campgrounds. Immediately we were good-naturedly assaulted with super-soakers filled with Faygo (if you miss the essentially good-natured manner in which business is conducted during the Gathering, it's easy to get scared or freaked out) and overwhelmed by the sheer number of homemade ICP-themed tattoos. Everywhere you went there were young men carrying crude cardboard signs reading, SHOW ME YOUR TITS. In other circumstances this message might be conveyed orally, but the Juggalos were taking no chances: They preferred what Cadence referred to as a multidisciplinary approach.

At every Gathering there is a plethora of brave souls carrying shabby cardboard signs begging Juggalettes to relieve them of their cursed virginity. At the Gathering, the mating dance takes on a new and radically different form. Subtlety, understatement, and gentlemanly wooing are out: Braying unashamedly for female flesh and/or a mercy fuck is in.

There was infinite variety behind this ubiquitous cry for the display of naked breasts. Within five minutes of hitting the Gathering, Cadence was propositioned twice. A gentleman on a stage next to the tent where Violent J and Shaggy 2 Dope would be giving what I liked to think of as a State of the Juggalo address had planted a sign into the ground reading

Hey,

So do u think you
have a nice rack?
Are you thirsty?
Show me your Tit-Tays . . . PleasE!
& Get a free drink
Its Hot Stay wet!
Whoop
Whoop!

To drive his message home, the enterprising gentleman included a smiley face, a childlike drawing of a glass of water, and a pair of smiling clown faces made up to resemble the professional guises of Shaggy 2 Dope and Violent J.

An even more enterprising young man flashed Cadence the requisite IF YOU SHOW ME YOUR TITS I'LL GIVE YOU A DRINK sign with a big Colgate smile. When she respectfully declined, he made an exaggerated frowny face and flipped over the sign so that it now read, AW, C'MON. I'LL GET YOU HIGH TOO! It was a real mark of Juggalo ingenuity that the youngster anticipated consistent rejection and had another offer on the table immediately. That's the kind of persistence that will someday land that young man in the White House. Other boob lovers in the crowd opted to mix a little autobiography into their appeal. A scrawny-looking African-American man wandered around with a sign pleading, FIRST GATHERING. PLEASE SHOW ASS, PUSSY OR TITS.

As is generally the case with Juggalos and ICP, there is no need to read between the lines or infer indirectly. The notorious infomercial for the 2010 Gathering spells it all out explicitly: "The magic in the air. The feeling of ten thousand best friends around you. The camaraderie, the family, and the love felt throughout the grounds. You'll meet people, make future best friends. You'll probably get laid. And you'll realize that the family coming together is what this is really about."

What lonely teenager doesn't want to hear that? Forget "family coming together": When you're a hormone-crazed teenager, getting laid *is* what *all* of life really seems to be about.

The copious free-flowing nudity on display throughout the Gathering made those poignant little signs exquisitely redundant. Immediately upon entering the Gathering we stumbled upon Ron Jeremy leading an aggregation of mostly naked Juggalettes being hosed with Faygo in a wet T-shirt contest. An audience of mostly male, video-camera-sporting rubberneckers looked on in open-mouthed appreciation as the women flaunted their tattooed flesh and raging lack of inhibitions.

Jeremy presided over the festivities with randy, cornball bonhomie. When two of the women began dancing next to each other, he leered, "By the way. Do you two know each other? Are you guys into women? Let's just see one little kiss, but you need to get your hands out of the way like in those porno movies. A little more tongue, one last kiss."

The porn legend was enough of a showman to realize that a contest like this needed more than just naked women being doused with Faygo; it needed elevation. So for the next round, the contestants were asked for their names and favorite sexual positions.

"Ashley. Doggy style," enthused the first contestant.

"Lindsey. Fucking from behind!" squeaked the second.

"The ass or the vagina?" Jeremy countered with an incongruous nonchalance that undercut the sleaziness of the question ever so slightly.

The rest of the girls expressed a pronounced preference for doggy style, but one contestant boldly established her individuality by bragging, "My name is Rook from Detroit, Michigan—Whoop! Whoop!—and I like any position except for boring because I am one erratic [erotic?] son of a bitch!"

In the next round, the women were asked to fake an orgasm in order to make it to the finals. "You've got to use your imagination because no one is tickling your vagina at the moment," Jeremy added with improbable matter-of-factness. He wasn't about to leave anything to chance: There would be no fatally confused competitors on his watch thinking, "Wait? I have to make an orgasm noise yet I'm not having an orgasm right now? How do I reconcile those contradictory facts? Oh the cognitive dissonance!"

One naked, heavily tattooed contender wasn't willing to rely solely on the powers of her imagination, so she began masturbating vigorously in front of the impressed crowd. Clearly, Jeremy's words were wasted on this fierce young future wet T-shirt champion. "This is called acting! Wait. I take that back. She's now diddling herself," Jeremy reflected as the woman enthusiastically fondled her pierced clitoris. An avalanche of faked orgasmic bliss ensued. I turned to Cadence and stage-whispered, "I'll have what she's having." I should probably mention at this point that this all occurred at about 3:30 in the afternoon.

The next contender went even further. After duly feigning an orgasm she quipped, "Oh, yeah, put your finger in my butt. Harder, harder. Wait, what's your name again?" Jeremy did not appreciate this encroachment on his territory. "That's right. I crack the jokes. You do the dancing. That's how it works. That's pretty fucking funny, though. 'Is that your finger in my butthole and what's your name?' You're a little wiseass, ain't ya? Someone take her home. She's ready."

Angry cries of "Take it off!" filled the air during the last dance, though at that point the Faygo-drenched young lovelies didn't really have anything left to take off. The gals were ultimately competing for the wet T-shirt contest's grand prize of seventy-five dollars in Insane Clown Posse merchandise, but the real reward lay in the performance itself. There's an unmistakable element of exhibitionism in being a Juggalo, in making a ridiculous spectacle of yourself no matter the consequences. The wet T-shirt contest represented this tendency in its purest form.

Jeremy was a quintessential Gathering of the Juggalos celebrity. He may be one of the world's most famous porn stars, but he was at the Gathering to serve as both a ribald, wisecracking host of the wet T-shirt and Miss Juggalette competitions and as a stand-up comedian at the Fresh Ass Comedy Tent. But he was mostly there as a personality, a showman, an entertainer, a quasivaudevillian whose banter and shtick were pure Catskills, albeit for a decidedly non-Catskills audience.

After the wet T-shirt contest, we ran into Jeremy and introduced ourselves and he more or less instinctively took a silver marker and signed Cadence's cleavage. She didn't ask him to do so but he did it anyway, because, well, when you're Ron Jeremy, that's what you do.

"Are you here primarily for hosting duties?" I asked.

"Well, that and I'm performing stand-up comedy though, did you guys see Hannibal Buress last night?" Jeremy asked of a genius black stand-up comedian Chris Rock has described as a cross between Dave Chappelle and Mitch Hedberg. Buress was already a critic's darling and a staff writer for *Saturday Night Live* when he made an unlikely exodus to Cave-in-Rock, yet he had performed at the Gathering as Ron Jeremy's opening act. He was still paying dues at that point, and some dues are stranger than others.

"I felt like a fool performing after him. If anything, I should be opening for him. I mean, I do what I do, but he's absolutely brilliant," Jeremy conceded. Offstage, Jeremy's razzle-dazzle professionalism gave way to something exhausted and dispirited. He had extraordinarily sad eyes. The following year we saw him lying nearly comatose in a chair in the stand-up comedy tent at four in the morning. Some teenaged Juggalos offered to get him high. "No thanks, guys," he told them as he stared off into the distance at nothing much in particular. "I'm just *tired.* I'm just tired," he continued. That tiredness seemed existential as much as anything.

Cadence and I then walked over to the Seminar Tent, where

Violent J and Shaggy 2 Dope were scheduled to deliver their yearly address to the faithful. (All of the daily talks between Psychopathic artists and their fans were given the strangely formal title of "seminar.")

I have come to see Violent J as the benevolent but absentminded stepfather to his Juggalo brood, and Shaggy 2 Dope as the fun uncle. In that respect, the annual Insane Clown Posse State of the Juggalo address represented the ICP equivalent of a long list of promises from Stepdad he'll never quite be able to keep.

In deference to the wishes of older fans, ICP announced it would be touring behind nothing but the old stuff and only be playing clubs without barricades so that there would be as few barriers as possible between the group and its fans, literally and figuratively. Even more excitingly, Violent J announced that at Hallowicked, the next card in the second Joker's pack would be revealed. This was a matter of utmost significance, as only one new Joker's Card had been revealed since Insane Clown Posse closed out the original set of six Joker's Cards with the revelation of the twin Joker's Cards *Shangri-La* and *Hell's Pit*: 2009's *Bang! Pow! Boom!,* the first Joker's Card in the second deck and a continual explosion that clears the souls of the damned from the Dark Carnival.

In a trembling voice, Violent J enthused, "I want to let everybody know, this Halloween night in Detroit, we will unveil the next Joker's Card. The name and image will be shown at Hallowicked this year at the same building, the Fillmore in downtown Detroit. We're not showing it everywhere on tour. For those live in person, this will come falling out of the sky. From the bottom of my nuts, the Joker's Card is extremely fucking exciting. The image has already been blasted into our fucking skulls. We know what it looks like. We know its name. It's so fucking energetic. I can't wait to show you the next album and the next Joker's Card. This is the second deck. Another six is what we're doing. We never thought after the first Joker's Cards that another hand would be dealt. But here we are. It's like we're living in the fucking future. This is 2010 and we're bringing the thunder. We wish we could make it drop now."

I found myself swept up in J's guileless enthusiasm and the equally guileless enthusiasm of the crowd. I got lost in J's wrestling cadences, the way he seemed to transform every sentence into a breast-beating boast, a self-deprecating dig, or some strange combination of the two. Wrestling was in J's blood. It was in his cadence, his swagger, his strut. It shaped the contours of his personality and public image just as indelibly as hip-hop did.

A furious tumult swept over the crowd as the assembled tried to bring this fabled new Joker's Card into existence through will alone. At that point people inexplicably started chanting for Violent J to take his shirt off. This was perplexing on multiple levels. Violent J writes in *Behind the Paint* that he has a terrible fear of appearing in public without his shirt on. At his seminar he elaborated with the following anecdote: "Quick story. One time we were doing a concert in Toledo and I was trying to do a backflip off the step. Let me set this up. This is way back in the day. I forget the name of the place. The Asylum. Something like that. Just packed. They couldn't move. You could walk over the crowd. The fire marshal showed up. So I do my ninja backflip over the top of the speaker set, and the next thing I remember I woke up in an ambulance halfway through a show. Cracked my head open and broke my collarbone in four places. But the real pain is they cut my shirt off. They carried me out in front of everybody with no fucking shirt. I'm glad I was unconscious. That was a horrifying and traumatic experience knowing my shirt was peeled in front of everybody. I was probably snoring. Ever see somebody get knocked unconscious and they're snoring? I had a nightmare about this very seminar last week. I dreamed I came out with no shirt and didn't even realize it."

Violent J insisted that nobody wanted to see him with his shirt off. No, Shaggy 2 Dope was the real sex symbol of the group, he proclaimed loudly. Violent J joked more than once that he was "two-thirds gay" for his group mate. To their credit, nobody seemed to make much of the statement.

Violent J announced that Insane Clown Posse was buying an old industrial building in Novi, Michigan, and transforming it into Juggalo Arena. Every other weekend, grapplers from Insane Clown Posse's Juggalo Championship Wrestling League would wrestle for free.

There would be after-parties and a television show and even a new album from the Golden Goldies, an Insane Clown Posse side project whose lyrics exclusively involve gold and gold-related items.

There was something incredibly humanizing about the lecture. Violent J echoed the sentiments of many of the assembled when he conceded, "I know we have a reputation of breaking promises and announcing things that don't ever happen. But if you check your fucking records, we're doing better. We've been coming through with our shit."

And that's all you can really ask for, isn't it? We aren't perfect, but we're trying.

If Insane Clown Posse institutionally had a reputation for breaking promises, it was in part because they promised so much. In 2012 Insane Clown Posse made its biggest and boldest statement to date when it promised to sue the FBI on behalf of its fans for designating Juggalos a "loosely organized hybrid gang."

To that end, Insane Clown Posse set up the website juggalos fightback.com, where fans who had suffered negative consequences because of their status as Juggalos could seek legal recourse through Insane Clown Posse's legal team. They also filed a lawsuit against the FBI over the classification.

The *ICP vs. FBI* scuffle underlines just how thoroughly fandom defines Juggalos: No one would ever imagine designating the fans of, say, Duncan Sheik as either a gang or a discriminated-against minority, because by all rights liking Duncan Sheik represents but a tiny component of someone's terminally beige personality, but to many people, hardcore Insane Clown Posse fandom is as central to a person's identity and sense of self as race, gender, sexual orientation, and religion and is just as likely, if not more likely, to lead to discrimination. The war of words between the FBI and ICP that kicked off at the 2012 Gathering brought the duo's eternal battle with the forces of cultural repression to the legal realm, but when I first set foot on the grounds in 2010 it struck me as an exhilaratingly lawless world, a new frontier where anything could and would happen.

The sense that all the rules and tradition that govern the non-Juggalo world had instantly disappeared was only strengthened by the revelation that many of the festival's top acts would be performing at four o'clock. In the morning. For example, Lil' Kim was scheduled to perform at Friday's "Ladies Night" at 3:20 A.M.

We quickly became acclimated to our surroundings. To get to the main stage where the marquee acts of the festival would be performing, you passed a series of tents and clubs housing seminars from Psychopathic artists, wrestling, carnival games, and, most important as far as many of the festival attendees were concerned, the infamous Drug Bridge.

Drug Bridge is exactly what its name suggests, a bridge where you could procure just about any illicit substance known to man. This was no furtive hideaway. There was nothing covert about it. There are window fronts in Amsterdam where women press their naked vaginas against the glass that are more subtle in their commercial appeal than the Drug Bridge. The idea is to advertise as blatantly as possible. Sometimes that meant literally yelling through a bullhorn or carrying a cardboard sign listing drugs for sale next to their respective prices. Sometimes you would see entire families selling bottles of prescription medication and feel bad for humanity as a whole. The Drug Bridge was to the Gathering of the Juggalos what the Lot was to Phish fans and Shakedown Street was to Deadheads: an open-air drug market, a dangerous and exciting place to be.

Cries of "Molly! Weed! Rolls! X!" could be heard everywhere. A girl held up a sign reading, FINEST BOSTON YAYO 70 BUCKS A GRAM WOOP! WOOP!

Spying the sign, a black security guard looked at it indignantly and asked her, "Seventy dollars a gram for some yayo? Damn, girl! Why you be trying to *rob* a Juggalo?" For days afterward, Cadence and I would ask each other, "Why you be trying to *rob* a Juggalo?" at random intervals.

For stoners and fans of sensory derangement, there's something extraordinarily exciting about the openness of the Drug Bridge. It takes the guesswork, scheming, and shame out of purchasing drugs. You don't need to know a guy who knows a guy who might be carrying: You just need to engage one of the many drug dealers loudly hawking their illegal wares.

During Insane Clown Posse's seminar the day that the shit went down, literally and figuratively, Violent J and Shaggy 2 Dope sent out exquisitely mixed signals about how its rabid fan base should treat Tila Tequila, the notorious MySpace celebrity, singer, and reality-show personality who was the most unexpected addition to the 2010 Gathering of the Juggalos lineup. On the one hand, Violent J acknowledged that it was funny as shit to watch somebody get hit with a dead fish or pelted with piss, and that Juggalos should feel free to behave however they see fit. At the same time, however, every performer at the Gathering was a guest of the Psychopathic family and should enjoy the same privileges afforded the Boondoxes, Anybody Killas, and Blaze Ya Dead Homeys of the world.

Shaggy 2 Dope offered a slightly less high-minded appeal. "I'm tryna fuck that bitch, yo! So don't be fucking it up for me," he insisted. If an appeal to family and graciousness and basic human decency didn't work, hopefully the crowd would be moved by the massive cultural force that is Shaggy 2 Dope's libido.

But before Tila Tequila performed a set that will live in infamy, Tom Green was scheduled to play an early-morning gig in the Fresh Ass Comedy Tent. He wasn't scheduled to go on until the early hours of the morning, but his starting time came and went with no sign of Green. This was not particularly unusual for the Gathering, where guests often came on dramatically late when they came on at all.

The crowd grew restless. Green was ten minutes, then twenty minutes, then a half hour late. The unrest grew more and more pronounced. A clown named Upchuck who served as an unofficial Juggalo mascot blessed and cursed with the job of introducing Green bore the brunt of the hostility.

"Fuck you, Upchuck, you fucking home wrecker!" yelled someone from the increasingly apoplectic crowd. "Because you fucked my wife I've got to pay two hundred dollars in child support a month, you wife-fucking motherfucker!"

"Hey, do you think Upchuck really fucked that guy's wife?" I asked Cadence.

"I don't know. I just know that it is heartbreaking to find the marital bed suddenly full of yellow synthetic hair and the sheets stained with clown makeup," Cadence replied.

Upchuck finally took the stage forty minutes after Green's set was supposed to begin and was immediately pelted with projectiles as he tried and failed to perform observational stand-up about dating. Nobody, it seemed, was interested in hearing about the romantic travails of Upchuck the Clown.

Upon taking the stage, Green immediately announced, "I'm taking the temperature of the room." He took a long, hard look at the crowd and adjusted his set accordingly.

We were in the land of white rappers, so Green rapped inter-mittently. Everyone in the audience was high, so Green got high onstage.

In between bong hits and hip-hop verses, Green cannily delivered a narrative the crowd could relate to. His tragicomic stand-up implicitly said, "I'm just like you. A Scrub. A Juggalo. Through some miraculous twist of fate, I was once one of the beautiful people. Through some cosmic fluke, I breathed the rarefied air of the Franklins. I had a show on MTV. I wrote, directed, and starred in a major motion picture, was referenced in hit songs, and married an unconscionably hot woman who also happened to be a huge movie star and a scion of one of the most prestigious acting dynasties in American history. Then everything went to shit. I got cancer. My movie was a flop. My show ended. Now I get drunk and host an online talk show in my living room and perform at three thirty in the morning in the middle of the woods." Like seemingly everyone at the Gathering of the Juggalos, Green was a survivor. The tumult of his personal and professional life had shaken him, but it had not destroyed him.

Like Violent J, Green had lived every scrub's dream, which lent an additional element of pathos to his set. He'd been to the top. Now he good-naturedly resided somewhere very different. It was a melancholy arc Green shared with many of the other acts on the bill. Vanilla Ice, Coolio, Slick Rick, Lil' Kim: They all used to be huge. Now they were just trying to get by.

"Does Drew Barrymore suck a mean dick?" yelled someone from the audience.

In most performances, a heckler who'd yell something like that would be angrily escorted out of a venue. Here it was a query that angrily demanded an answer, though I cannot remember exactly what that answer was.

After Green finished his casually triumphant set, we rambled on over to the Ladies Night tent to witness the debut Gathering performance of Tila Tequila. It promised to be a folly of epic proportions. It did not disappoint.

Like seemingly every other performer, Tequila came out an hour late to angry hoots and scattered projectiles. Violent J's wife, Sweet Sugar Slam, a Juggalo fixture and the mother of Violent J's children, introduced Tequila as an old high school friend. The desperation in her voice was palpable. Sugar Slam was trying to avoid the inevitable by presenting Tequila not as a controversial and reviled tabloid fixture but rather as a friend of the family. Heaven knows nothing resonates with Juggalos quite like the cry of "Family!"

A smattering of burly security guards formed a human wall of muscle for Tequila to perform behind once the projectiles started flying. The intense security measures became a self-fulfilling prophecy. They felt less like a deterrent than a challenge.

Tequila came out in a skimpy pair of Daisy Dukes and a bikini top. She was tiny, Lilliputian, even, and the presence of the lumbering men beside her made her seem even tinier by comparison. She looked like a miniature drag queen as she began performing selections from her new EP.

Just about everyone we'd spoken to on the ground that day predicted that something unfortunate would happen to Tequila that night. There was a dark, malevolent energy in the air all day long, though it was difficult to determine whether all the ominous talk of Tequila's imminent humiliation was Juggalo bluster.

The moment she came onstage, Tequila was met with a flurry of bottles and other debris from festival goers who had been drinking and smoking and drugging for hours. Earlier that day a Juggalo excitedly told us about the time he filled a soda bottle with urine and shit, then screwed the cap on loosely so that it would come off in flight when he threw it at Andrew W.K. He looked to repeat that performance during Tequila's set.

In an attempt to hold on to her fading dignity, Tequila would dart purposefully between her offensive line of burly security guards, peeking her head out and lip-synching a lyric before immediately racing out of the way of a projectile. Tequila wasn't a performer anymore. No, she was exclusively a target.

That's not entirely fair. She had other things to offer them as well. "Show your tits!" the crowd began to chant with more urgency and force than they'd chanted anything before. The cry was ubiquitous at the Gathering, but in this emotionally charged context it began to take on a menacing air. It was generally harmless, but the anger toward Tequila, however misplaced it might have been, felt visceral and real.

It was impossible not to empathize with this tiny little woman confronting a crowd that seemed to hate her for reasons she couldn't begin to understand. What could she do? The Juggalos' anger toward her wasn't rational. She hadn't done anything to hurt them. All she'd done was become rich and famous exploiting her sexuality.

In a bid to win over a hostile crowd, Tequila jeered, "I ain't no Paris Hilton up in this bitch! I'm not no Lauren Conrad. I'm real."

Tequila was attempting to communicate with the crowd through coded language. She was trying to say, "I understand. I know what it's like to have nothing. I know what it's like to have to remake yourself from scratch because the world tells you you're shit. I know what it's like to be hated and misunderstood by people who know nothing of me beyond the media stereotype. I wasn't born rich. I've had to fight for everything I have and I'll never stop fighting. People like me and you never do."

That is what Tequila was trying to say when she said that she wasn't Paris Hilton or Lauren Conrad. She was trying to establish, consciously or unconsciously, that she had a lot more in common with Juggalos than with heiresses and pampered reality-show princesses.

Tequila's performance became an epic battle of wills. Time seemed to slow down. Each song lasted an eternity. The fifteen minutes Tequila was slated to be onstage began to feel more like a week. Could she last? Would she make it through the set? Should she? "I'm right here. I'm not going anywhere," Tequila crowed in a supremely misguided attempt to impress the crowd with her toughness. Tequila faced an agonizing decision in that moment: Do you give in to a crowd that hates you, or do you try to win them over with your resilience and defiance?

Tequila chose the toughness and resilience route. It was a mistake. Combined with the confrontational nature of her songs, it lent an air of aggression to her performance the crowd responded to in turn. It was as if she were daring the crowd to live up to its abysmal reputation. The more Tequila said, "I'm not going nowhere!" the more abuse she endured. At one point Tom Green came out to do a silly little dance and serve as a decoy to distract Tequila's abusers.

Green's crowd-pleasing presence only slowed the abuse slightly. Like dogs, the crowd sensed fear and went in for the kill.

"Show your tits! Show your tits!" angrily demanded the crowd.

A panicked Tila Tequila threw off her top. It seemed a reasonable price to pay for this abuse to end. But the abuse did not end. It only slowed a little before it began again with great force and urgency. The fabled bottles of shit began raining down on the stage. Tequila was finally forced to admit defeat. She ran offstage. Juggalos ran after her in pursuit. They chased her to her trailer and overturned it. The next morning images of a bruised and battered Tequila were all over the news, along with her threat to file a lawsuit against Insane Clown Posse that would shut down the Gathering permanently.

There was an air of grim inevitability to the Tila Tequila affair. There was only one way this story was going to end, and it wasn't with Tila Tequila winning over the Juggalos. The problem wasn't necessarily that Tequila was too pop or too mainstream. No, Tequila went down because she failed to understand the situation she found herself in. Unlike Green, she had fatally misread the room.

Tequila wasn't savvy enough to discern the signs. Green was smart and experienced enough to realize that he was playing a venue unlike any other he'd ever played before and adjusted accordingly. He understood that smoking a little weed was a small price to pay for being accepted by a drunk, high crowd given a four-day exemption from having to follow the rules of man. He understood that "Whoop! Whoop!" meant "I understand and respect that you're very different" as much as it does hello. Tequila didn't understand the curious tribe she had been paid to perform before and suffered terrible consequences as a result.

That first day at the Gathering was so strange and surreal that what happened to Tequila didn't strike us as particularly remarkable or significant. There was only one way the shotgun marriage of Insane Clown Posse and Tila Tequila could end, and that was with a blood-splattered divorce. Tequila's violent removal from the Gathering was as preordained as any of the Joker's Cards. It was going to happen anyway. There was no use delaying the inevitable.

The following night, as we prepared to leave our Comfort Inn and descend into the heart of the Dark Carnival, a pair of burly, black, bullet-headed security guards accosted us.

"You guys are headed to the Gathering, right?"

"Yeah."

"I worked security there and I just got off an eighteen-hour shift, so I know how crazy things can get. You need to be careful, and I mean careful, if you want to get out of there alive. 'Cause a lot of people get stabbed there. One dude was just stabbed in the abdomen. Other people have been killed," one of the security guards assured us ominously.

"How can I be as safe as possible?" I inquired meekly, unashamedly taking the bait and giving in to the security guards' scare tactics.

The security guard had clearly given the matter a lot of thought. Speaking with absolute certainty, he instructed, "I don't know if you party or anything, but don't lose control of yourself or your surroundings. Don't buy anything on Drug Bridge. You never know where that shit came from or what it will do to you. Hold on to your woman at all times. Never let her out of your sight. Never. Stick to well-lit areas." Then, pausing and pounding his fist in his open hand for emphasis, he continued, "Whatever you do, what *ever* you do, don't go into Hepatitis Lake"—the not-so-respectful nickname for the campground's sketchy-looking lake. "It's called that for a reason."

It turned out all we really had to fear that night was the hateful invective of a prop comedian from the 1980s named Gallagher.

Bitterness, rage, and failure had transformed Gallagher into something crass and ugly and wrong. He had become a pop-culture Gollum. Bitterness and disappointment had poisoned his soul. Whatever light or humor he may have once projected had curdled into something sad and strange and hateful.

We sat outside the Fresh Ass Comedy Tent before Gallagher's performance began. I was struggling to regain consciousness after ingesting a regrettable combination of Molly, vodka, pot, acid, mushrooms, and, most disastrously, hash. A chubby, affable Juggalo had offered to share some hash with me if I'd let him use my pipe. Cadence shot me a stern look I unwisely ignored before officially ingesting at least one illicit substance too many. As darkest night entered the dawn, the Gathering became a blurry series of snapshots.

A scrawny teenager with sandy blond hair walked past us, bleeding profusely from his forehead, clutching a bat covered with barbed wire. "Are you okay?" Cadence asked.

"Yeah," he unsteadily but defiantly answered. "I mean, I'm just *expressing* myself."

At Insane Clown Posse protégés Twiztid's big headlining gig Saturday night, the duo announced that they always tried to plan something special for each Gathering, something to set it apart from a regular gig. So they were very excited to announce that, as a one-time-only treat, they would be playing their upcoming album for the first time in its entirety. Oh, they wouldn't be performing it live, mind you. No, they would be simply pressing a button and their new album would start playing over the loudspeakers.

A muted wave of disappointment swept over the crowd as it began to disperse.

This displeased some of the more loyal partisans. "C'mon, y'all! Where the fuck you going? This is Twiztid's new shit! No one else has even gotten a chance to hear it yet, and you are all walking away like some bitches!"

As we wandered away from the stage, we struck up a conversation with a couple selling dollar waters. "Aw, man," the man said, "when I get high, I mean *really, really* high, my son looks just like Ronald McDonald."

We wandered some more and came to a wrestling ring where

Officer Colt Cabana, a giant slab of toothy beefcake, informed the audience that they were all under arrest for a violation of Code 420 and would all be shuttled to prison imminently, where they would all be anally raped. Cabana was pitted against Weed-manJ420, a wrestler whose special powers involve his ability to smoke a fuck-ton of weed and still remain vaguely conscious. The next year we'd learn Officer Colt Cabana was a nice, college-educated Jewish boy from Wicker Park, but in that bleary moment he was simply one of a series of preposterous characters who floated into and out of my blinkered consciousness.

A light rain began to fall as Gallagher began to perform. In my stupid and stoned and decidedly nonsober state I began wondering why the space in front of the stage was completely bare. My acid-stoked cerebellum conveniently forgot the nature of Gallagher's act and obliviously assumed a front-row center seat would be ideal, or at the very least not the worst possible vantage point for any performer and/or any show, ever.

I was making one mistake after another. With a fuzzy head full of misguided confidence, I led Cadence to the empty spot in front of the stage. It was then that Gallagher and his helpers took a sledgehammer to a wide variety of sweet and savory substances.

In our bid to get out of the way of the rain, we placed ourselves squarely within firing range of whipped-cream pies, giant vats of mustard, and seemingly every sticky, gooey, staining substance known to man this side of Faygo Red Pop. In my drunken, fucked-up state I found myself thinking, "Sure this sucks. But it's got to end soon, right? So maybe if I just keep my composure and ride out this whole Gallagher-smashing-watermelons-

in-my-face-at-four-in-the-morning-in-Cave-in-Rock thing, I'll
be fine." So I waited. And waited. During this time my whole
body was inundated with an endless series of projectiles, each
more skin-crawlingly repulsive than the last. I finally felt, on a
physical level, what it was like to be a Juggalo.

But the physical discomfort was nothing compared to Gallagher's act, a bizarrely reactionary rant so overflowing with bile
and bitterness that it barely constituted speech at all, let alone
comedy.

If Tom Green appealed to Juggalos' innate vulnerability and
outsiderdom, Gallagher appealed to something much uglier: He
appealed to their sense of anger and resentment, to the sense that
their misfortune was directly tied to the success of people with
nicer clothes and tidier lawns. Of Obama, he whined, "He's half
black and half white. He's a latte. There's white milk in there. If
it's goat milk, he could be an Arab terrorist. He's got *bomb* in his
name!" It only went downhill from there. Gallagher's contempt
for the crowd was palpable. It was alienating. It was ugly. Finally
it became unbearable. For all its ugliness, there was an underlying sweetness and innocence to much of Insane Clown Posse's
world, a poignant longing for connection and family and acceptance and togetherness. There was none of that in Gallagher's
comedy. It was just ugly and hateful and wrong.

Cadence and I walked away in the light drizzle before the set
was over and took two chairs near the exit while we waited for
our chariot to pick us up and take us to the Comfort Inn. A Juggalo had warned us just before we prepared to leave that there
was a SWAT team near the entrance ready to make its move and

descend upon the Gathering with great force, but all we encountered was a single security guard passed out in a lawn chair.

Just before he dropped us off, our driver, the racetrack announcer with the golden voice and complicated history with John DeLorean, dropped one last bombshell. "I might want to check that festival out because"—he once again paused for dramatic effect—"two of my favorite hobbies are face painting and nudism."

Shit, the eminently respectable, silver-haired man was a secret Juggalo all along. He just didn't know it yet.

My first Gathering left me with a hunger for more. Next year, I vowed, we'd do the Gathering correctly, staying all four days and really immersing ourselves in the music and the lifestyle. We owed ICP that much. More important, we owed the Juggalos that much. I owed it to these strange and beautiful people.

It wasn't enough to go to the next Gathering: No, in order to really understand ICP, I'd have to travel to the spiritual home of the Dark Carnival in Detroit and celebrate the most profanely sacred day of the Juggalo year: October 31's Hallowicked.

A BRIEF, UNFORTUNATELY EMO CHAPTER IN WHICH OUR UNRELIABLE NARRATOR LOSES HIS SHIT AND FUCKS UP BIG-TIME AND ALSO, IN A REALLY STRANGE TURN OF EVENTS, BECOMES AN EMPLOYEE OF "WEIRD AL" YANKOVIC

By the time I set foot at my first Gathering, the focus of this book had shifted radically. A book about Phish that touched upon the seemingly antithetical but ultimately simpatico universe of Insane Clown Posse had morphed slowly but surreally into a book equally devoted to Insane Clown Posse and Phish.

My reasons for focusing on Insane Clown Posse were more emotional than journalistic, more personal than professional. When I set foot in Cave-in-Rock that August afternoon I had already experienced a devastating series of failures and fuck-ups that had put the future of this book in jeopardy. I had already spent part of the summer of 2010 following Phish without getting anything usable out of the experience. I had only myself to blame.

I have a remarkable capacity for alchemizing joy, happiness, and wonder into despair, depression, and misery. My antijoy machine transformed a gig so ridiculously sweet it still seems much too good to be true—spending a magical summer touring with Phish with my beloved girlfriend before the responsibilities of adulthood finally, climactically, and incontrovertibly crushed our youthful spirits—into something much darker.

I had fucked everything up but good. When I searched my soul I had to concede that I'd entered into the project with the wrong goals and the wrong motivation. I had convinced myself that the entire book was a valentine to Cadence, an opportunity for us to experience a treasured relic from her past together before we embarked on our new life together.

It was a gesture of love undercut by love's psycho sibling, obsession. It wasn't enough for me to have the woman of my dreams for the present and the future. No, I had to try to figure out a way to lay claim on her past as well.

In hindsight, it was a selfless gesture of incredible, even unforgivable selfishness. Cadence sensed that in writing this book I was looking for something that I was never going to find, that I was searching for something that no longer existed, if it ever had. I was not being honest with myself about my motives. It wasn't enough to simply explore something, to satiate my curiosity about human nature. No, there was something furtively avaricious about it. I had to lay claim to it. I had to make it my own.

I realize now that what I longed for more than anything was to experience the joy and the exhilaration I felt that New Year's Eve in Miami and throughout my first year with Cadence. I longed for transcendence, but my Jewish Midwestern brain told me that it was wrong to do so. If I was to seek out joy, I would need to do so under some sort of professional cover.

Joy was not for me. I couldn't simply go to a show and have a good time. No, I had to frame it in the soul-crushing vernacular of the pitch. I couldn't experience joy firsthand; I had to position it as a compelling sociological phenomenon.

So over the course of a very eventful day on June 25, 2010, I signed a mortgage, moved, signed the contract to write this book, and flew to the East Coast to catch a Phish show with Cadence the next evening.

Something was off from the very beginning as Cadence and I traveled about the country following Phish and chasing joy with fiercely divided spirits. There's something inherently melancholy about graduating from college and saying good-bye to your friends en route to a terrifyingly vague future. And now I was not only piloting Cadence's uncertain future, I was forcing her to contemplate parts of her past that she treasured but could never recapture.

Phish was a big part of who Cadence had been. It's still a part of her, but when I became obsessed with Phish it had already become a part of her life she was willing to let live happily in the past. Cadence had enjoyed her adolescence. Then she got over it. I, however, was hell-bent on vicariously experiencing Cadence's radiant adolescence even if it killed us both and destroyed my career.

Here's the thing about doing things for the wrong reasons: It always goes awry. The universe sees the deception and subterfuge in your soul and acts accordingly.

"I miss my friends. My friends aren't here," Cadence said to me during one show over the botched summer of 2010. I never understood the full portent of what she meant until now, as I write this well over a year later. Following Phish is a supremely communal experience, yet we were going it alone.

Rather than kick off our life together on a rollicking note, our nine 2010 dates with Phish were unmistakably bittersweet. All around us people were dancing and smiling and having fun, but they were not her friends, and she felt that absence acutely. I couldn't concentrate on the shows because all of my energy and attention were directed toward Cadence. That was entirely my fault. I had tunnel vision. I couldn't get out of my own head long enough to really empathize with or understand the people around me.

I had hoped to follow Phish throughout their 2010 tour and finish a book about it by the end of the year. That was the first of many disappointments, each more crushing than the last. I entered this project with an unforgivable lack of preparation, planning, and foresight. I just hoped that if I got out on the road something worth writing about would occur. I had faith in myself so utterly delusional that it bordered on madness.

I did not understand the Phish experience because I went in

under pretenses so false I damn near fooled myself. I wouldn't be able to write this book with a clear conscience until I was writing it from a place of emotional honesty. It would take me a solid year, oceans of abandoned prose, lots of fruitless trips and excursions, and tens of thousands of wasted dollars before I could do so. Writing books can be a tricky business when you have no fucking idea what you're doing.

I had to abandon plans to continue the Phish tour when it proved prohibitively expensive. I wasn't able to get anything out of the shows that I'd attended. I was there but I was still on the outside, still looking for a way in. I enjoyed the experience of going to see Phish. I enjoyed spending time in the summer outdoors with my girlfriend.

During that time my sense of self was shaken. I was overcome with fear that I would not be able to write the book I was professionally, morally, financially, and legally obligated to write. How could I when I had developed such agonizing social anxiety that the prospect of talking to a human being other than Cadence terrified me?

My life got a whole lot stranger when I got a Twitter message from my childhood hero "Weird Al" Yankovic announcing that after considering all the writers in the history of the universe, he had decided that I was the man to tell his story. He wanted me to write a coffee-table book about his life and career with him for Abrams Image.

It was an opportunity I probably should not have accepted. But I couldn't resist. How do you say no to "Weird Al"? How can you turn down an opportunity to work with your childhood hero? How can you disappoint a pop-culture icon? How can you tell a friend of children and misfits everywhere that you're too damned busy to tell his story? Who was I to say no to "Weird Al"?

You can't. You simply fucking can't. But accepting the gig of writing "Weird Al"'s coffee-table book meant that I'd be writing two books in a single summer while continuing to serve as *A. V. Club*'s head writer during a time of intense expansion, and, for me at least, mental disintegration.

Assembling the coffee-table book took my mind to some pretty strange places. I spent my thirty-fifth birthday in the living room of Jon "Bermuda" Schwartz, Yankovic's drummer, archivist, and webmaster, sorting through boxes upon boxes of seemingly identical photographs of Al from throughout the eighties and nineties. Schwartz saved and photographed everything: His garage has become a shrine to the man he has drummed behind for over three decades.

While poring through photo after photo in Schwartz's garage, I sank into what I call a "work coma." Time seemed to stop. The world around me disappeared. All that mattered, all that existed, was the work in front of me. I was able to block out the rest of the world even when I really shouldn't have.

On my thirty-fifth birthday I glimpsed into the abyss when a few errant drops of Coca-Cola seeped into my computer's hard drive and destroyed it. Rationally I understood that I was paying a terrible price for my carelessness, but my unconscious mind processed it as something much more sinister.

At the risk of being hyperbolic, I felt as if something cracked in me when my hard drive died. This anxiety manifested itself physically as a persistent twitchiness, a pervasive sense that unless I kept a constant inventory of my belongings at all times, they would all be lost or broken. If one thing can fall apart, then everything can fall apart. If everything can fall apart, then everything *will* fall apart.

I was retreating deeper and deeper into a prison of self. Yet even as I increasingly lost my grasp on reality, I came to develop an unexpected connection to Phish's music. I didn't notice it at the time, but the band's songs began to get under my skin, to affect me on an almost subliminal level so that when I encountered them again they boasted a new, unexpected resonance. My new affection for Phish's music and the subculture it inspired only contributed to the sense that I was failing not just myself, my editor, and my publisher, but my subjects as well: the groups and their pathologically dedicated fans.

In my paranoia, I was convinced that I had fucked up so badly and made so many terrible, unforgivable mistakes that the only people who could possibly accept me would be Juggalos, the most misunderstood and reviled people on earth. Juggaloism is on some level a celebration of failure, of fucking up, of being a scrub. I identified with Juggalos and Insane Clown Posse on a profoundly personal level. As this project flew off the rails and I entered an intense emotional downward spiral, that identification with the Juggalo aesthetic increased exponentially.

I felt like a failure. I felt like a weird, sad ghost of my former self. I felt broken. I felt fucked. I was feeling awfully Detroit, which was fortuitous, since that was where I was headed for Insane Clown Posse's 2010 Hallowicked hometown Detroit show.

THE CORRUPTION CONTINUES:
HALLOWICKED 2010

Detroit feels like the ruins of a great civilization. Once upon a time the city was the engine that drove our economy. It was the lifeblood of American commerce, a blue-collar utopia where a union man of modest means could buy a house and send his children to college on the wages he made working on an assembly line at GM or Ford or Chrysler. He could live the American dream, secure in the knowledge that because of his tireless toil, his good-for-nothing children could go to some hippie college and major in bong hits and Frisbee golf.

Then a series of cataclysms wracked Detroit. The Japanese came to dominate the automobile industry through sneaky, underhanded tactics like building better cars for lower prices. The American car industry entered a downward spiral from which it has yet to recover. Unions lost their clout. We moved from an industrial society driven by steel and oil and factories to a technology and information society.

Detroit failed to keep pace.

As society crumbled and the mighty institutions upon which Detroit was built lurched into irrelevancy, nothing took the automobile industry's place. Camelot morphed into a citywide Grey Gardens. The automotive capital of the United States began to look like the victim of a zombie apocalypse. The streets are strangely empty. Beautiful old buildings that once housed thriving businesses and families are covered with mold and graffiti. The ugly and corrupt have infected the gorgeous and pure. The city feels like a ghost town.

This is the world that created Insane Clown Posse. And Eminem. And Esham. And Kid Rock. And Iggy Pop. And Madonna. It's a world of poverty and shuttered buildings. The music Insane Clown Posse makes reflects that.

Is it any wonder Violent J developed such a vivid imagination? How could he not dream of something better? It's easy to see how one might develop a gothic imagination growing up in a dead city, surrounded by the rotting debris of a once-vital industry. If your life is going to suck, you might as well make an outrageous joke out of it. If you're going to be treated like a clown, then why not be the wickedest, freshest clown around?

It doesn't take much of a leap to look at the mean streets of Detroit and see a sinister circus. Acid rap and horrorcore thrived in a city so beaten down and desensitized that gangsta rap wasn't hardcore, violent, or strange enough for it anymore. N.W.A wasn't cutting it; that's where Esham and later ICP came in. What they lacked in polish or musicality they made up for in extremism and theatricality; they went too far, then kept on going. They transformed their lives into sick jokes, their everyday struggles into warped horror-comedy drive-in movies for the ears.

Yet there is something unbelievably pure about the devastation of Detroit today. It's as if one of the great cities of the world is being afforded an opportunity to start again from scratch on the ruins of a great civilization. There's a spirit in the air of rebirth and renewal, of hope and optimism. It's as if the fates are granting Detroit a giant cosmic Do-Over, a chance to rebuild on the faded glory of the past. Cadence and I fell in love with Detroit that Hallowicked weekend, with its potential, with its history, with its irresistible underdog spirit and gothic beauty. Like Cave-in-Rock during the Gathering, it was like no place on earth and the only place that could have birthed a phenomenon as doggedly strange and preternaturally resilient as Insane Clown Posse.

The line outside the Fillmore for Hallowicked 2010 was nearly a block long. Even on Halloween, Juggalos stood out. Orange-

and-black jack-o'-lantern face paint was nearly as ubiquitous as the signature greasepaint styles of Violent J and Shaggy 2 Dope. For reasons known only to himself, a young man was dressed as what appeared to be a gangsta ICP banana; he had a big, goofy banana costume festooned with the Hatchetman logo, yet nevertheless carried himself with swagger. He was fucking *owning* being the dude in the ICP banana costume at Hallowicked.

Behind us a cute, chubby, middle-aged black woman dressed up like a sexy cat reconnected with a man she bonded with during the 2006 Gathering when he had carried a sign offering "free hugs" and she happily took him up on his offer. Immediately in front of us, a man with a huge, menacing scar on his head that made him look like a bit player from *The Devil's Rejects* triumphantly told his friends, "For the first time in my life, I don't feel like a spectacle."

It was a statement of naked, poignant sincerity. He spoke for a lot of Juggalos. Three hundred and sixty days a year, they're the outcasts. But for five magical days every year, weirdness becomes the norm and normalcy becomes weird. The fringe becomes the mainstream, and the mainstream is reduced to the fringes. For five days it was all about Juggalove and Family and being embraced for your eccentricities and peculiar passions, not despite them. Hallowicked is much more conventional than the Gathering of the Juggalos. It may be ICP's biggest non-Gathering concert of the year but it is, in the end, a concert, whereas Gathering of the Juggalos is a world unto itself where the rules of man no longer apply, especially those involving drugs and nudity.

Juggalos are by nature a social genus. They travel in packs and luxuriate in the camaraderie and acceptance of their fellow Dark Carnival aficionados. Yet there was one man standing next to us who was very conspicuously alone.

The man turned around slowly and said to me, "Hey, you're Nathan, aren't you?"

I don't expect to be recognized anywhere, let alone in the line for an Insane Clown Posse concert in a city I'd never been to before.

The gentleman explained that he was one of the only other journalists covering the Gathering in 2010 and had been sent a link to a speech I gave about Juggalos earlier that afternoon.

He didn't quite look at me; instead he looked through me with spooky intensity. He had read my *A. V. Club* blog entry on the Tila Tequila attack online and clearly took issue with it for reasons he had difficulty articulating. "I mean, man, I read your piece online and uh"—he then paused and chose his words carefully—"it almost felt like you had a *problem* with what was going on with Tequila. Like that you found it *disturbing* or something."

Before I could explain that, yeah, there was part of me that was a little unnerved by a ninety-eight-pound woman being inundated with bottles of shit, he launched into an elaborate explanation of why he was at the Gathering. He was an old hand at festivals, an old-school "Burner."

"When I started going to Burning Man, it was all about freedom. You could do anything and I am, philosophically, all about what I call 'extreme freedom,' and that's scary for a lot of people. They can't handle it. They couldn't handle it at Burning Man. I mean, after that first year they wouldn't even allow you to have guns."

The man had come to the Gathering as part of an ongoing multimedia project about how festivals become universes unto themselves with a karmic energy and governing structure all their own. They were, in this gentleman's estimation, exemplars of extreme freedom where festival goers could enter an alternate universe for a few days where the outside rules didn't apply and drugs were a problem only if they were too expensive or not of sufficiently high quality.

Festivals were the Wild West, the last frontier, strange little quasi-nations of structured anarchy and free-floating chaos. The gentleman's philosophy was fundamentally libertarian; he didn't need a mommy state to tell him where he could or couldn't fire off guns or hurl projectiles at people in need of a spiritual awakening. The man had embraced the Dark Carnival with the zeal of the convert; he seemed to take the philosophy more literally and seriously than even Violent J himself.

"The message of the Dark Carnival and the Joker's Cards is to really examine yourself on a spiritual level. So when that happened to Tila that night, she was forced to come to terms with who she was as a person. Those pictures you saw of Tila on tmz. com, where she's got cuts and bruises on her face. That's the real Tila; that's what she looks like on the inside."

"So you're saying that Tila Tequila was moved to become a better person because of what happened to her at the Gathering?" Cadence asked incredulously.

"I dunno, man," he responded noncommittally. "That's on her, man."

As a hippie festival rat turned Juggalo, the man was the living embodiment of the interconnectedness of strange musical subcultures and the simpatico solidarity that each provides, yet I couldn't help but feel like in this man's eyes I was failing to live by the Juggalo Code.

The man was a spiritual seeker. In the Dark Carnival he'd found something that made sense, that reflected his own beliefs in karma and spiritual energy. I had become pretty obsessed with Insane Clown Posse myself. I was genuinely excited about the revelation of the second Joker's Card of the second pack and was way too geeked about the free EP Insane Clown Posse gives out at each Hallowicked.

I didn't suspect that another year on the road would transform me into a wild-eyed lunatic obsessed with energy and vibes and the interconnectedness of all things as well. I too would go upriver. The road would save me. It would also drive me mad.

Inside the Fillmore, we spied an Army armed forces recruiting table where a jarhead who looked like a deflated version of Dwayne "The Rock" Johnson delivered his spiel beside a pull-up bar. The juxtaposition of the marines and the Dark Carnival might strike some as incongruous, even surreal, but it's not the mismatch you might imagine. Violent J's beloved older brother Rob was a GI, and one of Violent J's earliest wrestling aliases was Corporal Robinson.

At Hallowicked, the army was looking for cannon fodder. What better place to find poor, undereducated young men with few resources or opportunities and an overwhelming air of desperation than at an Insane Clown Posse concert in Detroit?

While images of elite all-Juggalo units in clown makeup and camo filled my mind, Cadence asked the recruiter why the army chose this concert in particular to look for new recruits.

With an unmistakable air of defensiveness, the recruiter spat back, "What, soldiers aren't allowed to listen to Insane Clown Posse? We're looking for a diverse army, and there's an awful lot of diversity in this crowd."

I don't know exactly what I was expecting from ICP's Hallowicked performance, but I was initially underwhelmed by a set that looked as if it was borrowed wholesale from a cut-rate haunted house and a bunch of flunkies in cheap monster masks spraying Faygo into the crowd. I guess I expected an expensive, elaborate spectacle. This was Halloween, was it not? The most important, sacred day of the Juggalo year?

Then I realized that for Juggalos and ICP, a cheap haunted-house set and friends in monster masks spraying Faygo at an ecstatic audience constituted an expensive, elaborate spectacle. Hey, if it was good enough for the previous sixteen Hallowickeds, it was good for number seventeen as well. There was ultimately something strangely winning about the modesty of the duo's stage show. As big as the group has become, it never lost the low-budget feel of its earliest shows. It never stopped feeling homemade, intimate, like something that belonged to the fans more than the group.

The biggest anticlimax of the night had nothing to do with Twiztid. Just as Violent J had promised at the Gathering, Hallowicked marked the unveiling of the second Joker's Card of the second deck. Now, the concept of a *second* deck struck me as a little suspect. Like so much of the mythology of the Dark Carnival, the Joker's Cards have a split identity.

On one level, they represent little more than a clever sales gimmick. On another, they're the spiritual cornerstones of an entire makeshift faith.

Yet after the final Joker's Card was revealed, Insane Clown Posse went from being a group with a mysterious spiritual message to a pair of aging, weird-looking white dudes in clown makeup.

So they reupped for a second deck of Joker's Cards in 2009. This was problematic on multiple levels. The new album's title (and the first Joker's Card), *Bang! Pow! Boom!*, was both defiantly silly and suspiciously similar to the title of the Black Eyed Peas' single "Boom Boom Pow," a song with little if any spiritual portent.

The revelation of *Bang! Pow! Boom!* seemingly left nowhere for the second Joker's Cards to go but up, but when Violent J casually mentioned that they should probably get around to showing the second Joker's Card of the second deck, his tone hovered somewhere between nonchalant and mildly apologetic.

It was easy to see why when the second Joker's Card of the second deck was revealed to be . . . the Mighty Death Pop. When the Card was unveiled, I found myself thinking, "You're fucking kidding me, right? The Mighty Death Pop? That's the big revelation? You're really just fucking with us now, aren't you?"

"What were you expecting?" Cadence asked skeptically when I expressed my disappointment.

"I dunno, I guess, uh, the iconography of the first Joker's deck is at least interesting and evocative on an aesthetic level. The Ringmaster. The Great Milenko. The Riddle Box. Jack and Jake Jeckel.

Those are powerful and mysterious concepts. But *Bang! Pow! Boom!* and the Mighty Death Pop—those just seem stupid."

It was then that I realized that I'd become invested enough emotionally in Insane Clown Posse's career to be disappointed by them. It's only a slight exaggeration to say that I began counting the days until the next Gathering of the Juggalos. But I had a whole lot more to see and do before that could happen.

PHISH FOR REAL THIS TIME: MY BRAIN EXPLODES WITH JOY ON THE VERY FIRST NIGHT OF THE TOUR

I entered the fields of Bethel Woods on May 27, 2011, on the precipice of a complete emotional collapse. My body was turning against me. I couldn't sleep. I couldn't eat. I trembled with anxiety. I nursed fantasies of collapsing in a fetal ball and waking up weeks later, a new man. I thought about committing myself to a mental hospital.

I was losing my mind. My equilibrium was off. I had dizzy spells. I fell with disconcerting regularity. Anxiety and depression waged a fierce war for supremacy in my increasingly fractured psyche. I began to feel like I was about to lose my mind. I worried that I had experienced a profound and irreversible psychic split, that something had shattered in me that could never be made whole again.

I began to feel as if I were in *The Source Code*. It was as if the mangled corpse of my career as an author was in a room somewhere, yet my inexplicably functioning mind was still being sent off to run a series of increasingly insane-seeming and nonsensical errands for reasons I couldn't begin to understand.

I was suffering from a peculiarly twenty-first-century malady: an excess of awesomeness. I was simply doing too many amazing things at once. Separately, every aspect of my career exuded joy and potential. Together, it all somehow alchemized into something terrifying.

Ambition had been the engine that had fueled my career. But my ambition had turned on itself. Ambition respects only itself; it's never satiated, because satisfaction would defeat its whole purpose. It doesn't want the hunger to ever leave. It's always keen to remind us that the wolf is at the door and everything will fall apart tomorrow unless we push forward mercilessly in pursuit of the material possessions and professional accomplishments that inevitably fail to fill the hole deep inside you where love and self-acceptance should be.

I was convinced I would never be able to finish this book, that I would let down the profoundly good people whose faith in me

I now considered delusional. A massive tax bill had swallowed up my life's savings and put me deeply into debt. Bill collectors hounded me. The time I had taken off for this book, much of it wasted on pursuits and expensive trips that proved fruitless, jeopardized my position at *A.V. Club*. A book I hoped would bring me and Cadence closer instead was having the opposite effect.

I was headed for a fall. There were no two ways about it. My ego had gotten too big. I had lost touch with what mattered. I was pinballing madly toward oblivion. And now I was professionally, morally, and financially obligated to go out onto a road whose primal darkness I was convinced would consume me. They would find my battered corpse by the side of the road somewhere, identify me solely by my iPhone, shake their heads, and think that I just never should have left the comforting embrace of home. Cadence was the engine behind this book but I had to leave her behind because I couldn't afford to take her on the road and she couldn't afford to take the time off work or school. I was consumed with guilt and shame over the failures of the previous summer.

When I left for Phish's first show at Bethel Woods on May 27, 2011, I couldn't muster up the energy to maintain the illusion that I was following Phish as a responsible journalist with a story to cover and a book to turn in. I wasn't going to Bethel as an author or a journalist or a sane human being. I was a runaway. It didn't matter that I was thirty-five and running away from a life that should have filled me with joy; I was just another lost soul on the road in need of emotional rescue.

I had imagined that I could put one over on myself. My conscience knew better. When given a choice between the easy way and the hard way, it invariably chooses the way that might kill me.

In the strange summer of 2011, that meant heading out to follow Phish with almost no money, no car, no traveling companions, no real plans beyond hitting as many shows as possible without losing my job, a body riddled with anxiety and borderline paralyzing panic attacks, and a frazzled mind that could not see past October out of a strong conviction that at some point in the summer I would lose everything and crumble into nothingness.

It had been decades since I had felt so fragile and weak. I couldn't use Cadence as a buffer between an increasingly terrifying world and myself anymore. That had been the ruin of the botched attempted first tour. If I was going to survive the summer, I would need to become a kindness-seeking missile. I would have to lose myself and find myself. I would need to bleed. I would have to suffer. There could be no journalistic objectivity or distance; I would have to live the life.

I had never felt so powerless or doomed. The night before I left for Bethel Woods I held my editor and friend Keith's newborn baby in my arms for the first time and came close to weeping uncontrollably. I was half convinced that as long as I simply held on to this baby, this bastion of purity and innocence, I would be fine, but if I was to let go of the baby for even a second the darkness would consume me.

I entered the party bus transporting revelers from the Port Authority in Manhattan to Bethel Woods praying that the primal embrace of the crowd would save me, that it would set my rhythms right again. I was scared. I was freaked out. The prospect of attending a show without Cadence was terrifying. At that point, everything was terrifying. I liked Phish because I loved Cadence. With Cadence out of the equation, everything promised to be different. Different and weird.

I entered the bus alone. In every sense. A half hour into the ride the darkness began to crack and a light entered in the form of a goddamn lunatic from Milwaukee. In every group of friends, there is one buddy who is a little wilder and crazier and a little more out there than everybody else but also freer and more fun. The kind of friend you worry about and secretly envy. He or she is the rock star in the group, the wild card, the manic imp.

That clearly was Jared in his group of friends. A row or two behind me Jared and a fresh-faced kid from Milwaukee who looked unnervingly like the character actor Kevin Corrigan passed around a bottle of Seagram's Seven Crown and told strangers stories about some kids they knew who were "fucking *stupid*" in a way that made you really, really, really want to know what "stupid" meant in that context.

Jared had a spirit about him. He had charisma. He had magnetism. He had an aura. He was a rock star and a movie star even if he never touched a guitar or stepped in front of a camera. I went from thinking, "Who the fuck is this guy?" to "I want to party with this guy" over the course of about five minutes.

I would discover that Jared was an archetype you see at every show: the guilelessly enthusiastic (relative) innocent convinced he's about to have the best fucking weekend of his entire life. You know what? Oftentimes he does have the best fucking weekend of his entire life. His desire to party like no one has ever partied before becomes a strange, glorious, self-fulfilling prophecy.

It was sweet. Two twenty-something roommates from the Midwest were out for a big weekend in the big city. They glowed with excitement. Everyone did. If you were to make a map documenting levels of excitement, anticipation, and exhilaration in our country, I suspect you would find the densest, purest pockets of excitement, anticipation, and exhilaration in cities where Phish is playing.

Phish fans very visibly convey a level of excitement about their favorite band that outsiders find hard to fathom. No one needs to explain why people got excited about the Beatles. They were beautiful. They were brilliant. Their genius was self-evident. But people are flummoxed as to how a group notorious for playing endless versions of songs with titles like "Divided Sky," "Fluffhead," and "David Bowie" could inspire such feverish devotion. There's something downright un-American about getting so goddamn excited about a band that means nothing to the vast majority of the American public.

At the epicenter of the Phish experience lies the tantalizing promise of instant friendship and freedom from judgment. If you grew up feeling lonely or weird or ostracized, the idea that people will inherently like you just because you enjoy the same music as them is incredibly powerful and appealing. That's true of Juggalos as well. If anything, it's even more true of Juggalos.

But it went far beyond that. Most rock 'n' roll shows promise a good time. Phish shows offer the possibility, if not the promise, of transcendence. It's not just the music but rather a strange, hard to quantify combination of music, history, drugs, and nature that combines to make a truly ecstatic Phish show not just a concert but a borderline spiritual experience. It also involves really great fucking acid.

That was the key that night at Bethel. Jared, the Kevin Corrigan look-alike, and I didn't leave the bus so much as we raced deliriously to the venue. Upon hitting the Lot, we encountered a shirtless man whose tattoos clearly marked him as a native of Detroit. He saw the look of excitement and anticipation in our eyes and immediately made it his business to hook us up with whatever we wanted.

It's a curiously ubiquitous custom at Phish shows: You meet an absolute stranger who intuits what you need and makes it his immediate goal to fill it. There's often a mutually symbiotic nature to the exchange, since chances are the goal you both share is scoring Molly or doses.

Whatever the reason, a shirtless guy with Detroit tats decided that it was of the utmost importance that I and some other dudes he had met five minutes earlier secure the drugs of their choice.

There was an instant chemistry between us, both because we were fucked up and because we were all from the Midwest. I had once believed that the Internet had rendered geography irrelevant. If you can send ideas and energy out into the world, then why should it matter where you are physically?

That now seems naïve. Of course geography matters. Cities matter. Cities get in your bloodstream. They tell you who you are. They're in your soul. They define you.

For the purposes of the conversation we were having, that definition was incredibly literal. I was Chicago. Jared—or Golden Child, as I would come to think of him—and his best friend Kevin Corrigan's doppelgänger were Milwaukee, and Detroit, well, Detroit was Detroit. It was written in ink on his skin.

He had a Detroit kind of personality as well: tough, funny, a bit of a hardass, but underneath obviously a good, decent, salt-of-the-earth-type motherfucker.

He was fucking funny as well. "Dude, I fucking love my girlfriend but you have sexy fucking eyes. I bet you're dating someone way out of your league," Detroit told the Golden Child.

"He is," answered Kevin Corrigan's doppelgänger.

"Not the girlfriend, but the girl I am fucking is really fucking hot," the Golden Child clarified.

Detroit wasn't backing down. He was going all in.

"I'm not saying you're gay or anything but I bet there are times when you're drunk and you see those eyes and start thinking about women," he said to Kevin Corrigan's doppelgänger while somehow managing to retain his air of brawny Midwestern machismo.

Detroit let the matter rest, but there was no denying that this was a sexy motherfucker. Kevin Corrigan's doppelgänger had a full-time job on his hands at Bethel Woods keeping him from fucking every woman who smiled at him. At Bethel Woods every woman and a number of men smiled at him. With intent. How could you not? The energy he was sending out into the world was unbelievable. He was rolling, having the kind of night that he would never forget if only he was able to remember it.

"Dude. I like your fucking T-shirt. I will trade you for it," barked Detroit as he pointed to my Creation Museum T-shirt reading, PREPARE TO BELIEVE.

I fucking love that shirt, but the one he was offering in exchange was arguably even sweeter: a dingy, dirty, caricature of Frank Zappa.

It felt like karma. Cadence loves Zappa, or at least she did back in her days of youthful passions, so the shirt felt like a talisman. It would keep me safe. It would protect me from sinister spirits of the road. Between the incredible purity of a newborn's innocence and the iconic weirdness of Zappa, I had it covered. I was set.

I loved the Creation Museum shirt because it had a history. It had character. It was an indelible document of a surreal trip Cadence and I had experienced to the epicenter of creationist self-delusion. Cadence and I were driving down to North Carolina when we saw a sign advertising the Creation Museum. At the exact same time we looked at each other and said simultaneously, "We need to pull over and go there."

The shirt told a story. When I traded it for the Zappa shirt, the story became Detroit's. He might not know the story. He may not care. But it's there all the same.

We were trading old stories for new ones. I was trading in the story of the Creation Museum for the story of how I met a strange and awesome man from Detroit in the parking lot of a Phish show in Bethel Woods, fucking Woodstock, man, and traded a T-shirt I loved and meant something to me for a shirt that meant something important to this man.

Monetarily, the shirt was worthless. It literally had almost no value. Its value was entirely sentimental, abstract.

I need more things in my life with completely intangible value. I had driven myself half insane chasing an impossible mirage of professional success when what I was really hungering for was human connection and life experiences. I had gotten it backwards. I imagined that if I achieved enough professional success, human connection would follow. Turns out it doesn't work that way. You can't expect people to come to you, no matter who you are. You need to meet people where they are, on their terms.

Detroit started passing around a beer that quickly became community property. Everything became community property in the Lot at Bethel. I had forgotten that.

Before I knew it, I had secured Molly and doses. Oh, but these were no ordinary doses. If the brown acid at Woodstock has become lazy shorthand for bad drugs, then the LSD seemingly everyone in the state of New York and I consumed during Phish's first show at Bethel was its inverse. If the brown acid was evil incarnate, then this LSD should have had angel wings. Fuck, I'm not sure it didn't.

It does not seem at all coincidental that seemingly everybody at the show that night was on the same killer batch of LSD. It's damn near impossible to understand the Phish experience without understanding LSD, for the Phish experience and the LSD experience are inextricably intertwined.

LSD and Phish shows each traffic in the beautiful illusion of international brotherhood, in the gorgeous if unfeasible belief that we are all united in some strange existential sense, that we're all passengers in the same great cosmic journey. This illusion becomes palatable because everyone at a Phish show generally is on the same wavelength. Their minds are open and hungry. They experience a sense of community with everyone around them rooted in music but also in drugs and memory and nostalgia and a history so fierce it takes on an almost physical presence.

LSD is central to the Phish experience in the way it twists and distorts and stretches time. To outsiders, the idea of a twenty-minute jam to a song with a title like "Divided Sky" or "Fluffhead" sounds like torture, but Phish fans have patience. They have to. If they don't have the patience to follow Trey's muse wherever it wanders, then they're probably not going to be Phish fans for very long.

That first night in Bethel I issued a series of silent prayers that the band would never stop playing, that we'd all grow old and die and Trey, Mike, Jon, and Page would still be up there onstage rocking out.

When I entered the venue, the woods came alive. The overwhelming sense of dread that had overtaken me for months was replaced by sheer exhilaration. I experienced an inexplicable surge of pure joy. This strange concert in this city and venue I'd never been to before began to feel like the best kind of home.

Everyone around me exuded a complementary sense of joy. This was it. It was the moment we'd all been waiting for. The ceremony was officially about to begin all over again. I found myself filled with an incredible sense of anticipation. It wasn't just that I had come to enjoy Phish's music as a by-product of my overwhelming love for Cadence: I fucking needed to hear these songs. I needed to hear this music. It was fucking essential.

The world took on a radiant glow. The LSD was speaking to me. I experienced a full-on epiphany. The woods and the concert and the road and the LSD were all letting me know that while the road contained darkness and peril, it also contained joy and wonder and light. The woods and the concert and the road and the LSD were letting me know that while *I* contained darkness and peril, I also contained joy and light. There was a small but distinct chance that my world would not end in October, as I had so desperately needed to believe. There was even an outside chance that I might make it through my little adventure alive.

I had left Chicago in a state of existential darkness, but everywhere I looked I encountered light. That's the great thing about Phish shows for the painfully shy and self-conscious: People will talk to you. You don't even necessarily need to strike up a conversation: People just need to talk. I just needed to talk. I still do.

There was a sense that in the primal, nurturing wilderness we could cast off all the bullshit and compromises of the corrupt outside world and be our best, truest selves. We could return to a place of innocence, of purity. This was no mere rock 'n' roll show. This was paradise. This was Eden.

By the time we entered Bethel, Kevin Corrigan's doppelgänger was well on his way to losing his friend. He couldn't help it. His friend belonged to the show now. Like beers and pipes and stashes, he had become communal property as he ricocheted madly around the show in a state of ecstatic joy. He lived to be part of the crowd. Later in the bus he recounted how he would find himself in the front row and wonder how in the hell he got there. On the bus ride over, he giddily recounted how he'd run onto the field twice during a Milwaukee Brewers game. There was no real rhyme or reason behind the action, just the eternal adolescent's "Looky me, looky me!" Alas, he had the kind of daft sweetness that made "Looky me, looky me!" not only bearable but strangely charming.

By that point the Golden Child was lost to me as well, but I did not feel alone. For Golden Child and Kevin Corrigan's doppelgänger are what I have come to see as Phish friends. Phish friendship is a strange and often beautiful thing rooted, as you might imagine, in a shared appreciation for the music of Phish and the mind-expanding properties of marijuana, LSD, mushrooms, and Molly.

In that respect, the Phish friend is a lot like the proverbial drug friend. The overlap can be tremendous and dispiriting. I know that over the course of my trip I always felt a little sad when Phish friendships morphed slowly but surely into drug friendships. Phish friendships, for all their drugged-up decadence, are at least rooted in the sense of community and life that comes with following Phish. Drug friendships all too often consist of two people tricking themselves into thinking they're less alone by sharing their vices.

Phish friendships are often defined by their ephemeral nature; it's not at all unusual to meet someone at a Phish show, take drugs with them, experience a fierce emotional connection, vow to remain in touch, then never see them again or catch a fleeting glimpse of them a few shows down the road. Actually, that's something of an ideal Phish friendship. Linger too long and the magic has a way of dissipating.

Time is relative in Phish World. Just as a song can seemingly last a day and a concert a lifetime, it's possible to have a wholly satisfying friendship with a fellow Phish fan that begins and ends over the course of a single hour.

An example: As I stood there in the comforting blackness, listening to Trey and the band perform music I was convinced the universe had commanded them to play, a handsome young man in his midtwenties tapped me on the shoulder.

"Dude, I don't know why, but there's this big empty space right behind you. I'm gonna dance in it."

I confess that in my narcissistic, grandiose delirium I looked back at the empty circle behind me and thought that I had fallen into such a dark place mentally that my negative energy had manifested itself physically as a meteor of blackness in this most sacred of hippie cathedrals.

I began to think of the blank space behind me as My Darkness. It's ridiculous, of course, but I felt oddly proud.

If this was really *my* darkness, if it truly was a physical manifestation of the ugliness and tension and pressure in my soul, then there was something beautiful, even sublime about the idea of an exuberant stranger dancing madly in it. He was even polite enough to ask permission before doing so.

A sheen of sweat coated his handsome face as he whirled about madly next to a girlfriend who wasn't just beautiful but radiant. He was drunk and a little out of control and crazy with joy and she very maternally made sure he was properly hydrated and looked after and cared for. Eventually, we started talking.

"You want a story for your book? Here's a story. A guy finds Phish in high school, he parties, goes to college, goes to work for the man, but still comes to shows for release."

He was spinning a familiar narrative: You find Phish. It changes your life and rewires your circuitry, you grow up and do the college, job, marriage thing but you still go to shows now and then because it's part of your history, it's part of your past, it's part of who you are.

The man worked for a defense contractor, but he wanted to do more. He wanted to do good. We all did. We wanted to prove ourselves worthy of the unimaginable bounty we had been given.

He was looking for something to believe in, someone to serve, a cause to devote his life to. He could be forgiven for imagining that the answers to the questions throttling his soul could be found in a field in Bethel Woods. That night we all could.

In that field we were reborn. We weren't just concert attendees. We were spiritual seekers in the midst of a transcendent experience. We were beckoning spirits. We were asking deep questions. We were seeking wisdom.

The more alienated from the world I became that summer, the more I employed the royal *we* in my writing. I apparently felt that if I professed to speak for all of humanity at once, then maybe I could secure a backdoor entrance into the brotherhood of man. In the fields of Bethel Woods, however, I finally felt qualified to use the royal *we* for the first time in forever. I felt like I could speak for everyone around me and everyone around me could speak for me.

Us. There's something powerful in the word and in the idea. I had fallen into a pit of isolation in Chicago. I had disappeared so deeply and painfully inside myself that nobody even seemed to notice my soul had gone missing, including myself.

The universe was saying: This is not about you. My narcissism said, "Everything is about you."

The man's girlfriend offered me kettle corn. I took a handful and said, without irony or self-consciousness, "You're like an angel!"

She enthused, "I *feel* like an angel!"

"You remind me of my girlfriend's sister Romy," I told her. "She also has a really great energy about her."

"I know! My sister is from Romania. This is her first Phish show. Isn't that great?"

In its own way, it was the perfect response. When I looked at them, I saw Cadence and myself. I felt connected to everyone.

When I told her about the book, she told me she'd worked as a publicist but was going back to school to be a social worker. "I teach ballet to children with disabilities. They don't understand any of that bullshit about money and power and all that other shit. They just understand beauty."

She handed me her card, but it seemed like not just an empty but a counterproductive gesture. Tonight was all about shaking off the strictures of the outside world, of abandoning a world of business cards and promotions and anxiety and chasing that Big Joy.

We made plans to hang out the following day, though neither of us expected those plans to come to fruition, and with that our curious friendship came to an end. I doubt they remember meeting me. I'm not entirely sure reading this would even jog their memory. It was that kind of a night.

I should probably reiterate now that I was on some incredibly powerful acid at that point and probably could have had an intense, engaging, and, in my mind at least, important conversation with a sea urchin or owl or spore of some sort. Instead I ended up talking with a pair of nice Vermont academics in their midfifties who were sitting on a blanket behind me staring into the glorious void, their pupils dilated, their minds expanding rapidly.

When Phish played the Talking Heads' "Crosseyed and Painless," as they did throughout the first leg of the tour, it triggered a flood of sense memories. I was instantly brought back to the Hanukkah at the group home where I grew up. Alumni of the system had given me three tapes that would go on to have a huge impact on my life and career: De La Soul's *3 Feet High and Rising*, Matthew Sweet's *Girlfriend*, and the Talking Heads' *Sand in the Vaseline*. I was instantly catapulted to the first concert of my adult life, David Byrne at the Vic in Chicago, as a seventeen-year-old. My body remembered countless nights spent half watching the Talking Heads' *Stop Making Sense* and *Storytelling Giant* during my years as a video-store clerk. A flood of memories, all of them positive, was unleashed by Phish covering a song I'd heard countless times.

I no longer felt as though I was watching a mere concert. I felt as though I was experiencing a profound spiritual epiphany about the fundamental benevolence of the universe. I couldn't have been the only one. I felt a tidal wave of LSD-inspired spiritual epiphanies that night. The epiphanies weren't limited to that particular show.

Time stretched forward and backwards. I felt connected not just to Phish but to the Grateful Dead scene that birthed it. Throughout the woods, people were experiencing epiphanies. A twenty-two-year-old was realizing he didn't have to go to law school just because his family wanted him to. Or maybe he was realizing that being a lawyer wouldn't be so bad as long as he was able to write and play guitar on the weekends. It felt as if the show that I was attending was no different from Woodstock or a Grateful Dead show in Boston in 1979. It was all part of the same continuum, the same trip. I had hopped on board late, having zealously hidden my inner hippie for decades, but now I was most assuredly part of that world.

That night changed me. I was no longer someone who enjoyed going to Phish shows because his girlfriend was a fan. Phish now had a much deeper meaning for me.

If Phish's music is rooted in Trey's magical guitar, its mythology is grounded in stories. Those stories don't necessarily revolve around the band. Nine times out of ten they revolve around the fan. Every Phish fan has that ultimate Phish story, that time they risked losing their job or skipped their best friend's wedding or gave up an opportunity to make a lot of money because it was more important for them to drive fifteen hours with their buddy to hit some show that would live forever in their memories, growing more legendary and epic with every successive year.

These are stories of devotion and commitment, tales where the dictates of Phish World outstripped those of the outside world.

It would not be enough for me to simply hear some of these stories or document them for posterity: No, I would need to live some of these Phish stories myself. I will forever be grateful to Phish—and, more specifically, to their fans and the world their fans created—for saving my fucking life that night, for lifting me out of a bottomless depression and showing me that the world contained more than rejection, failure, desperation, and sadness.

Something clicked in me. It was as if this concert, this fucking rock 'n' roll show, had somehow intuited that something deep within me was broken and healed it instantaneously.

That sounds ridiculous, I know. A few years back I would have sneered at the very notion that a concert could have that impact. I don't have those kinds of defenses anymore. The road broke me down. That night in Bethel Woods I began to feel as if the road was starting to build me up all over again. It was reminding me that while there was darkness in the road, there was also light. There was joy.

The Golden Child unsurprisingly nearly missed the bus. He was passed out on the ground somewhere when someone recognized him and brought him back. He was lucky. Suspiciously lucky. He was the kind of guy who could be dropped from the top of the Empire State Building and land in the arms of a bikini-clad supermodel covering her head with a bag of acid-soaked hundred-dollar bills.

The Golden Child was also spinning. Hard. I had taken one roll of LSD, seen God, experienced a spiritual epiphany, and had my DNA rewired. He had taken seven hits of the same acid, so I can only assume he had seven times as intense an experience. His pupils were the size of quarters. His unsteady gaze was fixed nowhere in particular.

He was so lost that Kevin Corrigan's doppelgänger tried to lure him back with the soothing reassurance of the familiar.

"I'm not the dude. *You're* the Dude!" he smilingly told the Golden Child for what must have been the thousandth time. It was like a private language between them, their own Dude-speak. The Golden Child smiled but needed additional reassurance.

"Would you like to listen to some music?" I asked before handing over my iPod. It was a way of paying it forward.

So I gave him my headphones and experienced that giddy surge of satisfaction that comes with doing something good for another human being. For the first time in as long as I could remember, I felt connected: to someone, to something, to the whole gestalt of Phish in that moment. It felt good. It felt right. I wanted that feeling to linger as long as humanly possible, despite knowing that its power lay in the ephemeral.

THE TOUR CONTINUES AS OUR HAPLESS PROTAGONIST TRIES TO FIGURE OUT HOW TO OPERATE WITH A BLOWN MIND AND LEAKING SKULL

I could barely sleep that first night back after the bus dropped us all off back in Manhattan. I just stared at the shadows of my dingy little hotel room with Phish songs bouncing through my mind. I wanted to call Cadence and tell her about the night but worried that I lacked the eloquence to put my experience into words. I was still rolling pretty hard.

I managed a few hours' sleep before I was back on the bus to Bethel. The Golden Boy and Kevin Corrigan's doppelgänger had opted out for the evening, so I planted myself in front of the most charismatic dude on the bus and hoped I'd be able to find a way to shoehorn myself into his conversation.

It turned out to be a wise move. Behind me sat a man who bore a distinct resemblance to Jesus (in a good way) and an attractive woman I learned was a flight attendant for JetBlue with a degree in anthropology. They were not a couple. She had been turned on to the scene by a boyfriend she was no longer with (she volunteered just a little too aggressively), but by this point she was a zealot. Her Phish fandom had nearly cost her jobs and relationships, but she wouldn't trade a minute of it. Like a lot of Phish fans, myself included, she had the zeal of the convert.

The Jesus look-alike had a longer relationship with Phish. He'd gotten into them in high school and throughout his teen and college years Phish was the epicenter of his social scene. He'd graduated from the University of Pennsylvania and was in the process of working on something that combined the uncanny powers of GPS with the unholy acumen of the iPod, in addition to funding and running a satirical website. He was, in other words, the living refutation of the notion that pot, or at least the accouterments of the hippie lifestyle, kills ambition.

Yet he'd never lost his affection for Phish. In a hectic and stressful life, it was a release valve, something he could do a couple times every summer to reconnect with his younger, wilder, more carefree self. I was impressed, in no small part because he was so oblivious to his attractive seat partner's advances.

Once we hit the ground, I set about the very undignified task of tagging along with the Jesus look-alike as he wandered about the Lot.

"You can follow me if you'd like," he told me, which was good, since I was going to do it anyway.

Nitrous was a controversial fixture of Phish shows. While the police in each city tended to turn a blind eye to pot and designer drugs, they seemed to take special pride in busting nitrous dealers. Their zeal was understandable: Nitrous was dirty, it was extraordinarily public (there's simply no way to make a giant tank of gas inconspicuous), and, worst of all, it was not something that I personally enjoyed, the ultimate mark of any drug's ultimate worth.

"An interesting arc for your book might be coming into the whole scene as an outsider and then falling in love with it," the Jesus look-alike said offhandedly.

"Yeah. That already kind of happened. Last night. I had kind of a religious experience."

I then wandered over to the nitrous tank area with the Jesus look-alike and I semi-inhaled some balloons before we wandered over to the man's friends and I discovered that this was no mere Phish fan I had been hanging with. No, I had spent the previous two hours with a gentleman whose existential identity will forever be Slow-Talking Hippie Guy from *Survivor*.

That, friends, is pretty fucking impressive. I'm so goddamn insecure that I cannot meet someone without thrusting all of my books and press clippings into their arms, yet this infinitely more secure, rugged, and successful soul could just casually let slip that he was an iconic figure on one of the most successful reality shows of all time. The experience had scarred him; after the show ended, he had to wrestle with very nearly winning a million dollars only to come home empty-handed.

After the show the man said, "Phish has been unusually tight. It's like they've been doing yoga together or something," which, for better or worse, is the kind of thing you'd imagine the slow-talking hippie guy from *Survivor* might say, Ivy League education or not. He also said the editor of *Survivor* was flummoxed because he said a lot of insightful, incisive things during his time on the show but he said them at a prohibitively slow pace.

The Jesus look-alike's buddies were all extremely smart and had wicked-thick Boston accents. So when they'd say things like, "I really like reading historical fiction. Lewis and Clahk wahr total badasses, and I'll read anything Stephen Ambrose wrote," it struck me as amusingly incongruous even though it shouldn't have.

Though the Jesus look-alike could be profiled as a Phish fan from a thousand feet away, his buddies cut more traditionally jockish figures.

One of them was sober. It was of course a long road to sobriety, one with more valleys than peaks. Once upon a time, this gentleman explained, he was just like all his buddies. He loved to party and he loved Phish. He raged and raged and raged until he somehow found himself surrounded by heroin addicts and crackheads. Partying with his friends had led to a heroin addiction.

With just the right note of pitch-black self-deprecation, he delineated exactly when things changed, when fun stopped being fun and became perilous, if not deadly.

"It's hard to party when you're fucking using needles."

He went on, "I just said to myself, how did I get here? A crack house, broken needles in my arm. Nobody liked me. *Nobody*. And that killed me. 'Cause I'm a social animal. And suddenly the only people I'm hanging out with are fucking junkies in the back room of a shed and they're no fucking fun.

"It got bad. Fucking syringe in the heart. It got fucking ugly, it did."

The man cut a melancholy figure. He was a cautionary warning of the dangers of riding the high too hard for too long. So going to Phish with his friends was a profoundly bittersweet experience.

Like everything in the world of Phish and, if I may extend the analogy a little, the history of the universe, it's not all good and bad but a furious combination of the two. So when the man looked into the rearview, he saw four overdoses and broken needles and lost nights in crack houses but also wicked fucking awesome nights when Trey and the boys seemed to be playing only for him.

The journey ended with him sipping a can of near beer in a beer cozy while his buddies hunted for Molly, but the journey there was worth it. In the words of Kris Kristofferson, the coming up was worth the going down.

The third night at Bethel, the Golden Boy and Kevin Corrigan's doppelgänger returned. It's always fascinating watching friendships from the outside, and I was touched by the tenderness of their bond. Kevin Corrigan's doppelgänger had fallen on some bleachers a while back and had been racked with seizures that kept him from being able to drive. Then one day the seizures stopped. He was all better.

"It's amazing how something as simple as being able to drive a car can make a huge difference in your life," Kevin Corrigan's doppelgänger observed with a spirit of Zen serenity. Earlier, the Golden Child had claimed credit for the seizure stoppage: "We moved in together and then, bam, they stopped!"

At Bethel that third night I met the third musketeer in their little group, an uptight business student who knew the Golden Boy and Kevin Corrigan's doppelgänger from Milwaukee. He had never experienced a Phish show firsthand.

It was fascinating experiencing Phish World through a newcomer's eyes, though it didn't take long for him to grow comfortable. Phish World is a different universe of one-dollar grilled-cheese sandwiches and glassy-eyed acid casualties, but it can also feel familiar and warm and inviting pretty quickly.

My quest for Molly proved less fruitful than my quest for the demon's brew known as Four Loko. I should have known better. Nothing good ever comes of drinking Four Loko, not even getting drunk.

The stranger next to me saw me staring intently at a man selling Four Loko and tried to scare me off it, warning, "Don't fucking drink that stuff. I drank that shit last year. I was puking up blood. For hours. For hours." In retrospect that man was my half-assed guardian angel. If only I had listened to him.

Four Loko isn't just bad for you. Booze is bad for you. Caffeine is bad for you. Four Loko, on the other hand, is fucking evil. Toxic. Satan's frothy essence.

What is it about Four Loko that makes it such a force of pure evil? It's just malt liquor and caffeine, yet somehow after ingesting a few you find yourself wondering how exactly you ended up boxing a bull naked in front of an arena of enraged spectators.

In my case I went from "How bad could it really be?" to "Why is my brain bleeding?"

I bought my can of Four Loko, rejoined the Golden Boy and Kevin Corrigan's doppelgänger, then joined a herd of people racing madly to get to the concert as Phish bashed out the exhilarating first chords of "AC/DC Bag." I was in a terrible hurry. I needed to be where the noise was, where the music was, where the joy was, where the people were.

With Four Loko coursing through my veins, I was feeling no pain. I was part of an ecstatic herd giddy with excitement and anticipation over the grand finale to Phish's Bethel Woods run.

I was rushing too fast and I tripped. I tripped hard, plummeting to the hard concrete face-first. I broke the fall with my forehead and my glasses.

I was dizzy. The world was spinning. Blood gushed out of a giant gaping open wound above my left eyebrow.

All around I could hear startled, horrified cries of "Oh shit."

Everyone around me was feeling my pain.

I staggered back to my feet and walked a few steps before *bam!* I was on the concrete and marinating in my own blood all over again.

"Stay down! Stay down!" a stranger called out as I lay woozy and bleeding on the hard concrete.

"I'm not gay or anything, but you should hold on to me till we get to the paramedics' tent," the Golden Child said as he locked his arm in mine. That's one of the nice things about Phish shows. People are always looking out for each other. So while there are always going to be people going too far—going too far is kind of what a Phish show is all about—there are also going to be people trying to reel them in.

In the medical tent, a grandmotherly medic asked me for my name and address. Great. Now there was going to be a legal document attesting to the inconvenient fact that of all the drunk, fucked-up revelers at a Phish show, I was the one that needed help. I was *that* guy, the guy people pitied and felt sorry for.

"Not that I care, but how many drinks have you had, hon?" the woman inquired soothingly.

"Just two, but one was a Four Loko." I paused and reflected on my atrocious judgment. "Fucking Four Loko."

I looked down at my shoes. I had tripped because I was losing my sole.

The symbolism of the moment couldn't have been more obvious.

I had been heading for a fall for months now. I was working too hard, eating too little, drinking and smoking too much pot, never exercising, obsessing darkly over a book I wasn't sure I would be able to write and a future I was convinced was completely fucked. My life had been thrown off balance. Everything seemed off. I felt incredibly vulnerable emotionally, professionally, and financially.

And then it finally happened. I cracked my fucking skull open at a Phish show.

There is something strangely liberating about experiencing the worst-case scenario and surviving.

The guy who had impressed me with how ridiculously fucked

up he was when we met two days earlier was now looking at me with brotherly concern.

Yet the fall had not killed me. Dazed me? Sure. Was I in agonizing pain? Of course. But I was a survivor, my daddy's hardheaded little boy.

"Now, sugar, you're probably going to want to go to the hospital in Bethel Woods. You're looking at three stitches at least. If you don't have that taken care of immediately the blood might glue the left eye shut," the angelic medic informed me.

I sat in the medical tent in a profound state of humiliation and disorientation. The nurse affixed gauze all over my bleeding eye and forehead until I looked like a deranged hippie sheikh.

I had only been following Phish for three days that tour and already I looked like a complete lunatic.

"Do you want to go to the hospital or do you want to stay, honey?"

My choice was clear. I could either go to the hospital and receive much-needed medical attention, or I could stay and watch Trey shred. It was a defining moment.

When I hit the ground my first thought was, If this doesn't kill me, Cadence will. That's all I cared about. I could live with the pain and the bleeding and the ugliness. I could live with looking like a mangled maniac for a few weeks (two, it turned out). That seemed weirdly honest. I couldn't live with Cadence fretting about her bloody boyfriend in a tent a thousand miles away, helpless, manic, and bleeding.

"I'll stay," I announced dramatically. I had chosen. I had chosen Phish over my health and sanity. I looked like someone just barely holding on.

I had ignored all the warning signs. I had ignored that saint of a man who had spent hours puking up blood after drinking Four Loko. Even more remarkably, Phish had tried to warn me. "Cavern," the third to last song Phish had played the night before, ends with the lyrics, "Whatever you do, take care of your shoes."

Maybe it was the sinister remnants of the Four Loko; maybe it was the light-headedness induced by the massive blood loss I had suffered, but Phish sounded absolutely amazing that night. The irresistibly catchy "Suzy Greenberg" never sounded tighter or more playfully mean-spirited. The Lynyrd Skynyrd cover "The Ballad of Curtis Loew," with its affectionate portrayal of a hard-drinking bluesman, never sounded so soulful.

The second set was even better than the first. "Simple" was, appropriately enough, elegant in its simplicity; for a guitarist who usually plays with such strenuous virtuosity, it was refreshing to hear Anastasio bash out some chords, though he did of course afford himself time for a lengthy solo. He wouldn't be Trey if he didn't. "Joy," with its heartbreaking fragility and aching sincerity, spoke powerfully to the quivering vulnerability I'd been feeling since well before I left for Bethel Woods.

The night before, the Slow-Talking Hippie Guy from *Survivor* had adroitly said, "Trey's ego is the force that drives the band. He wants to be the best guitarist in the world." For Anastasio, that is a reasonable, attainable goal, so there was considerable irony when Trey sang, "And you know I play a bad guitar" on a perfectly shambling rendition of "Loving Cup" that night.

"Loving Cup" ranks as one of the all-time great drinking

songs, yet Trey is one of pop music's most famous recovering alcoholics. Drugs were much of the fuel behind Phish's rise and enduring popularity, yet they were also the force that nearly destroyed them. Trey had to get sober so that the carnival of light could roar back to life and an army of fans could get fucked up watching a sober man play guitar. That is the duality at the core of the Phish drug experience; you can buy a popular KEEP TREY SOBER sticker only a few feet away from places where you can buy drugs. Hell, there's a very good chance you can buy drugs *from* the vendor selling you the KEEP TREY SOBER.

I realized I'd reached a tipping point in my Phish fandom when I began to start thinking about, and referring to, the members of the group by their first names. Usually I'd find that obnoxious, but if you're going to see a band something like twenty-nine times, as I did over the course of my misadventures, you begin to feel a sense of intimacy with them.

I felt like a fool. Much of the left side of my face was black and blue and gushing blood. I looked like I'd gone ten rounds with Mike Tyson. For at least the next week everyone who encountered my mangled visage was like, "Dude, what the fuck happened to your face?"

Inside Phish World, my gesture looked less retarded than heroic. Or at least I had deluded myself into thinking so. I was the fearless fucking warrior who wanted to see Trey and the boys play so badly that he couldn't be dragged away from a concert even when he was basting in his own blood.

I prefer the Phish World version of events because it makes me seem less sad and desperate and more like a dude who just loves to fucking party, even while bleeding profusely from the head. *Especially* when bleeding profusely from the head.

My mind raced. I was doing something very, very stupid and self-destructive. I should have done what the nice woman suggested and take a little trip to a lovely country hospital where I imagined a nice doctor with a corncob pipe would fix me up nicely and send me merrily on my way, but I couldn't leave this joyful madness, this ecstatic frenzy. And the journey had only really just begun.

The Golden Child and Kevin Corrigan's doppelgänger returned to the real world and Milwaukee after Bethel, and the Slow-Talking Hippie Guy from *Survivor* slipped back into Phish World for but a single show, so when the morning came I had to figure out a way to get from the enchanted woods of Bethel to the next show in the decidedly nonmagical burg of Holmdel, New Jersey.

So I went back to the Port Authority in Manhattan and was cha-grined to learn that the good people of Greyhound did not travel to Holmdel. In fact, Phish seemed to have deliberately set out to play venues not reachable by Greyhound. Greyhound would be my chariot throughout my voyage, so that posed something of a problem. Thankfully, a nice man with a cab looked inside an ancient little book and ascertained it would cost me exactly one hundred and six dollars to travel to Holmdel, plus tip.

So I traveled to Holmdel and told the cabdriver to take me to the nearest hotel. It was a really nice Comfort Inn, though it clearly took everything in her power for the clerk checking me in to keep from blurting, "What the fuck happened to your face?" I appreciated the restraint. If I let it, my mind would replay the fall over and over again, reliving that fateful moment when I lost control and went splat against the merciless concrete like it was Satan's own instant replay.

The first thing I did when I got to New Jersey was throw my accursed shoes in the trash. My soul was hopefully not beyond redemption, but the sole of my shoe certainly was. I briefly considered burning them in a sacrificial frenzy but thought better of it. Besides, where would I even start a fire?

I really began to miss Cadence. The rush of that first night in Bethel started to fade, and I ached from the fall.

I wanted to send out the friendliest possible vibes at the Holmdel show, but my black eye and giant scar gave me an aura that was less hippie chill than "enraged homeless man with big mouth and no left hook."

All around me people conveyed joy. People always radiate joy at Phish concerts. That's what makes them so irresistible to fans and so insufferable to everyone else.

But my joy was back in Chicago, and as exuberant as the people around me might have been, they were strangers. Thankfully, even strangers are friends at Phish shows. Or at least friends with weed. Never in my life have I encountered people so free with their weed, and I lived in a college co-op for two years and have covered hip-hop for fifteen. In Holmdel a skinny boy with shaggy black hair asked if I wanted to smoke a joint with him.

I nodded. "How old are you?"

"Seventeen."

"Good Lord. I'm old enough to be your father."

"Yeah, my dad's somewhere in there," he said softly, and pointed at the pavilion.

"Have you been a Phish fan for a long time?"

"This is only my third show. I'm really into the Dead. Furthur is more my scene, and this is more my dad's scene," he said of a father somewhere on the premises.

The show was a veritable youthquake. In the bathroom I stood in line for the urinal behind a red-faced, jubilant college student who couldn't have been over nineteen. "Oh man, oh man, oh man," the baby-faced teenager said to the person pissing next to him in a manner that suggested an LSD trip.

"You have *got* to read *The Portable Nietzsche*," the teenager continued. "I read that book freshman year and it literally changed my life."

"You might also want to check out some really swell Wittgenstein primers while you're at it," I piped in unsolicited, feeling moderately ashamed of myself for being a smartass during a time like this.

"That would be great 'cause my philosophy professor at Tufts is one of the world's preeminent Wittgenstein scholars," he piped back enthusiastically.

I am not going to pretend that this Wittgenstein-loving eighteen-year-old is the typical Phish fan. But he wasn't as much of an anomaly as you might expect, either.

On the road everything seemed intensified. It was as if upon my thirty-fifth birthday I folded in on myself and regressed back to being a wild-eyed, faintly unhinged seventeen-year-old. I lost my ability to function in the world. I felt incapable of making small talk. The character in pop culture I identified with the most was Michael Shannon in *Revolutionary Road*. Don't nobody want to be that guy, myself included. There was some weird, manic part of my brain that thought I should go into people's homes and expose the emptiness and superficiality of their bourgeois existences for them. As a public service. For their own sake as much as my own. I had no time for trivialities and social niceties. I was after the messy, unvarnished truth.

Before I left for Bethel, all I could see was the darkness and ego and dysfunction in myself, so all I could see was the darkness and ego and dysfunction in other people. I wanted to connect with others but remained locked in the prison of self. Thankfully, Phish World sent me down a lifeline.

As I was leaving my hotel in Holmdel, New Jersey, en route to parts unknown, an acid casualty in his early sixties with the grizzled, worse-for-wear look of someone who had been on the road way too long shot me a very purposeful look.

"Dude, are you Rojas's friend?" the man asked a little too insistently as he sized me up with inexplicable wide-eyed wonder. He shot me a look that said, "I know you and I know what you're up to." I reciprocated with a gaze that hopefully conveyed just as succinctly and unmistakably, "No you don't."

"No," I replied forcefully.

The man was not convinced. He continued to shoot me an incredulous look, then glanced over at the hotelkeeper behind the counter for backup, as if the puzzled woman might provide concrete confirmation that, protests to the contrary, I was indeed Rojas's friend.

"Are you sure, man? Are you sure Rojas didn't give you that black eye?" he continued.

Rojas did not appear to be a very convivial colleague. Nor did his friend. Their friendship was, at the very least, troubled. It did not take a DEA agent to figure out what line of work Rojas and his friend might be in.

"I guess that makes sense, 'cause if you were Rojas's friend you wouldn't be carrying that"—he pointed at my suitcase, a bulky silver-and-white number with a busy design that looks like it belongs to a wealthy dowager in a Marx Brothers movie—"you'd be carrying two fucking huge cases like this."

He then pantomimed carrying a pair of extraordinarily, even comically oversized suitcases before finally, conclusively determining that I was ultimately not Rojas's friend and consequently of no interest to him.

This was another kind of Phish story. An archetypal Phish tale, in a lot of ways: sketchy dude in a tie-dyed shirt and a ponytail whose mind has been blown by way too much acid and whose life is one giant fuzzy misadventure.

He'd been on the road for what appeared to be decades. It had taken its toll. During my travels, I encountered a lot of long-in-the-tooth Phish fans who, to paraphrase Gram Parsons, had grown kind and wise with age. This man was not one of them.

I took a cab to the nearest Greyhound station, in Newark, New Jersey. The weight of abandoned dreams and ruined lives hung heavy over it.

You could cut the desperation with a knife. Even Greyhound's slogan, "Fly Greyhound," betrays its low self-esteem and inferiority complex. United's motto is never going to be "United: Like Taking the Space Shuttle Without Ever Leaving the Stratosphere."

Greyhounds are a world unto themselves. They look and smell and feel like no place else. There is a strange texture to the air itself, a punishingly antiseptic quality. Greyhound buses are wonderful places for the curious and shy to eavesdrop on the gregarious and excessively public. Behind me on the Greyhound that night, a twenty-year-old white spitfire talked to an elegant older black man with a voice so soothing and sonorous it might have lulled me to sleep if the mismatched duo's banter didn't render sleep an impossibility.

She liked Katt Williams and Kevin Hart and Dane Cook, she told the older man as he listened attentively, but she really liked Ron White because he reminded her of her daddy.

Her daddy called her Spazz and taught her how to fight.

The older man listened patiently. He exuded an air of quiet assurance that made you wonder what in the hell he was doing taking a Greyhound bus from Newark.

Everybody who rides a Greyhound from Newark at that hour might as well wear a sign reading, ASK ME ABOUT THE HORRIBLE MISTAKES THAT HAVE LED ME HERE.

The girl had managed to pack two millennia of activity into two decades of living. At twenty, she announced dramatically, she was finally ready to settle down, if only with herself.

She'd been through it all and just barely survived. She'd been to jail. She partied, fucked around with drugs, got strung out on heroin, and kicked it herself. No rehab, no nothing. Just lying on a fucking floor and crying and shitting herself until the poisons finally exited her system. She was tough. Bitches around where she lived knew not to fuck with her, she reported sternly.

She had a reputation, she announced with pride. People where she lived knew not to fuck with her or they'd get knocked the fuck out. She'd done her time. She had her scars, literally and figuratively.

The girl said the n-word with remarkable ease and regularity despite being white and in conversation with a black man who clearly would never use the phrase himself in any context.

She said she used the word because she felt so at home with black people. To her, it was a badge of her familiarity with African-Americans. She didn't seem to have any conception that the word was poisonous because nobody around her seemed to see it that way. She believed that the word had lost whatever dark power it might once have possessed, either through time or ubiquity or sheer overuse.

She said she smoked pot because it calmed her rages and helped her sleep. She had kicked all other drugs but she was never going to stop smoking weed.

Oh, you will someday, he assured her paternally.

No, I don't think I ever will, she responded.

The two were flirting while continuously asserting that they were not flirting, found the practice of flirting dubious, and had no interest in each other physically despite repeatedly complimenting each other's looks.

"You must have been a real player back in your time. You must have broken a lot of hearts back in the day," she purred.

"I did all right," he said diplomatically, but when he looked back at his own life he was filled with regret.

He had turned it around and was looking to make a transition from being a corrections officer to a motivational speaker and author. He spoke hypnotically of the differences between the corrupt material world and our spiritual lives.

He had reached an important place in his spiritual journey and wanted to share what was inside him with the world.

These two were as much a part of the trip as anything else; the sleeping long-haul trucks by the side of the road and the elegant lady behind the ticket counter in Pittsburgh who looked a little like a young Eartha Kitt and had her hair and nails done up perfect and played some half-forgotten soul song on a small boombox that somehow transformed her little corner of hell into Motown circa 1966.

It was all part of the experience, the weird spiritual communion with great cosmic American music and great American people.

The pair got off in Pittsburgh after promising to keep in touch.

As if on cue, a black man dressed in all white got on board. He had a thick red scar along the left side of his face the same muddy red color as the pupils of his dilated eyes, and he sat down next to me.

Scars would be a recurring motif throughout my travels. From the deeply scarred man at Hallowicked who announced that for the first time in his life he didn't feel like a spectacle to the beautiful scar I picked up in Bethel Woods and now this man, who looked at the massive scar on my face and sensed a kindred spirit.

Pointing to my eye he joked, "I think we know the same guy."

I smiled, then feigned going back to sleep as the deeply scarred man began mumbling in what seemed to be a cracked-out haze.

Then it happened: The slurred, semicoherent rhymes gradually began to take the form of raps.

These weren't popular songs; they were unmistakably his own compositions.

I'm not sure the man even knew that he was rapping out loud. It was possible that he imagined that he was still engrossed in an endless internal monologue.

It was another side of the great music gestalt: the unknown, the undiscovered, the never-was whose career peaks at freestyling on a Greyhound bus at five in the morning. In his raps he called himself a young Jay-Z and a young Gucci Mane despite clearly being in his midforties.

I was impressed less by the content of his rhymes than by the obvious thought and care that went into their presentation.

I half opened my eyes just enough to see that the man next to me had pulled out a stack of ripped notebook paper and was performing the raps he had scribbled down in indecipherable blue ink.

This was the written part of his performance. At a certain point he started freestyling. I know this because he clearly demarcated which of his raps were written and which he improvised on the spot.

In its own way, it was a complete show: the established numbers, some freestyles, and some shout-outs to his boys SwaggaB and Li'l Wizel.

So Swagga B and Li'l Wizel, you can take comfort in the knowledge that your man didn't forget you that night. You were in his thoughts. You were in his dreams. You were in his rhymes.

His work done, the man then drifted off to sleep. There was an almost embarrassingly intimate element to the performance. It was as if I had stumbled into the man's waking dream.

Like all graduates of the Chicago public education system, my knowledge of geography is limited to a vague understanding that the United States might be in the Western Hemisphere (It is, isn't it? Please check on this, Scribner fact checkers!), so I had only the vaguest notion of where Clarkston, Michigan, might be in relation to Columbus, Ohio, where Greyhound vomited me forth following that sleepless fourteen-and-a-half-hour bus ride.

After failing to secure lodging at a shitty, reasonably priced hotel—there was a big science fiction convention in town that had monopolized the vast majority of the city's available hotel rooms—I ended up at a Hyatt far beyond my pay grade where I attempted to sleep and "eat" and orient myself and do various things people do in order to feel human.

After a deep, restorative sleep, I wandered downstairs, where corpulent Darth Mauls and teenage Klingons congregated happily in the hotel bar, giddy to be among their own. They were another kind of pop-culture tribe, as distinct and colorful in their own right as Juggalos and Phish fans.

I stepped out into a glorious summer afternoon and went to a convenience store to buy beer. The softly drawling cashier behind the counter looked at the scrawny, vulnerable-looking make-pretend Jedi in front of me in line and said poignantly while selling him sodas and energy drinks, "Treasure your youth while you still have it. It'll be gone before you know it. And protect yourself. Protect yourself. People around here can be so cruel."

The young man shrugged indifferently. He was, after all, a teenager.

"Where are you from, sir?" I asked the cashier while he rang up my beer.

"Oh, I'm from around here. That's how I know that people can be so cruel," he replied with a tragic lilt in his voice.

The next night I was back on track. I made the two-hour exodus from Columbus to Akron (mere minutes from Cuyahoga Falls, the jewel of northeastern Ohio!) via Greyhound and took a cab to the Blossom Music Center. Just before we entered the parking lot I panicked, and, convinced the cab would be searched, ate an entire gram bag of Molly before I got out.

Big mistake. Dumping such a large amount of Molly into my fragile system all at once made my body temperature rocket upward and my face turn an unhealthy shade of red. I looked like I was on the verge of heatstroke because I probably *was* on the verge of heatstroke.

"Stay cool, Nathan. Stay cool," my interior monologue sagely cautioned as I set out in fruitless search of a nearby reservoir of water I might submerge my entire being into. Despite my condition, as soon as the opening notes to "Kill Devil Falls" kicked in, a surge of visceral excitement swept over me. The adrenalized, infectious "Kill Devil Falls" was always a great way to begin a set, but it seemed especially appropriate given the venue.

Even by Phish standards, the band played a spectacularly goofy set that night. Phish's sense of humor was markedly different from my own. It was often childlike (they were, after all, a band that sometimes performed in unison while jumping on trampolines), and while I might once have listened to the comedy endemic both to Phish's original songs and their choice of covers (that night Phish covered Allen Toussaint's "Sneaking Sally Through the Alley" and Little Feat's "Rocket in My Pocket," both of which are about as somber as their titles suggest) and thought of it, to paraphrase the *Onion*'s description of the comical hijinks in the *Star Wars* prequels, as the kind of thing "fans have come to know and tolerate," I was no longer in a place where I prized or valued my sense of humor or aesthetic or taste or sensibility above anyone else's. Phish's sense of humor was a huge part of what made them Phish (just as Insane Clown Posse's antithetical but still very central sense of humor represented a huge part of what made them Insane Clown Posse), and at that point I had embraced Phish in its entirety.

The more I saw Phish that summer, the more parallels I saw between Phish fandom and baseball fandom: the more all-American a pastime following Phish became. Baseball games and Phish shows each stretched on for about three hours on average and thrived on the in-between times—those leisurely moments when a batter steps out of the batter's box and stares absent-mindedly into the stands while swinging his bat, or when Phish explores the notes in between the choruses and the climaxes. They were all about congregating with like-minded souls, birds of a feather who flocked together to take Molly and rage out or drink beer in the sun with buddies.

Baseball fans and Phish fans each had to have faith that the same eminently fallible group of men—our guys—doing the same goddamn things over and over again, night after night, can bring tremendous pleasure even if nothing remarkable happens. But there's also the exhilarating possibility that something extraordinary will occur, whether it's a four-home-run game from some slugger or a triple play or Phish playing a song they haven't played in ages and might never play again. That night, for example, Phish played a punkishly bratty curio called "Fuck Your Face" it has, as of this writing, only played five times in its history, as well as "Rocket in My Pocket," which it had played only once before.

Both baseball and Phish fandom were about tradition, about friendship, about camaraderie, about being unhealthily fixated on the performances of absolute strangers. During my travels I'd occasionally run into men my age who were on tours of major league baseball parks with their fathers, and it always struck me as a strangely simpatico exercise to following Phish with friends. Both were, on some level, about solidifying and reaffirming bonds rooted in shared passions and histories, and both had a weirdly statistical element to them. Throughout my travels I encountered fans who made great sport out of predicting the first song Phish would play and their subsequent set list. There was a science to it, it appeared. It was the Phish-fan equivalent of fantasy baseball or Bill James worship. For me nothing took the joy out of something, especially something so primal and emotional as music, quite like adding mathematics to the equation, but for some fans this only increased their enjoyment. Where I once saw Phish fans as a homogenous mass of stoned, hippie-dancing space cadets, I now saw infinite variety in their ranks, though some folks are easier to peg as Phish fans, as my guide for the next chapter in my adventures would illustrate.

TWO FOR THE ROAD: OUR NARRATOR FINDS A TEMPORARY TRAVELING COMPANION

You can generally spot a Phish fan one of two ways: They're either someone who looks really, really fucked up or they look open-minded, curious, and bursting with energy and excitement. The two are of course not mutually exclusive. Oftentimes Phish fans are open-minded, wildly curious, and bursting with energy and excitement about getting really, really fucked up. And oftentimes someone who ends up looking really, really fucked up began as an open-minded, curious kid bursting with energy and excitement.

That was true of a gentleman I first encountered at the Phish show at the Blossom Music Center. On my way into the venue, I locked eyes with an intense-looking young man with dirty blond hair, electric blue eyes, and a skeletal frame who appeared to be sweating violently from every pore of his body. We looked at each other just long enough to be concerned that the other person was way too fucked up. An empathetic cry of "Are you all right, dude?" may even have been uttered. Then we passed like two proverbial sickly, messed-up dudes at a Phish show. On ships. In the night.

I reencountered the man at an Ohio bus station, where I would be taking the bus to Cincinnati for that night's show. Our individual trips had overlapped before we had even been properly introduced, though being properly introduced at a Phish show can be a quixotic endeavor, since the person you're introduced to is probably not going to remember you. Oh, sure, they'd like to. I would love to remember the names of even half the wonderful people I met on tour, but it's just not possible. I'm not sure if it's even advisable. Linger too long and the moment fades.

"You going to the show?" I asked by way of introduction. He replied affirmatively.

Like mine, his summer had become one long act of incoherent improvisation with the universe. He'd lost his license after getting a DUI and was traveling light with just a felt bag and a few essentials. He was, of all things, a bill collector in real life despite being in massive debt himself, so he was riding both sides of the karma train.

Before I left for the open road that summer I had fallen into such deep debt myself that bill collectors were calling my employer with dire warnings of what might happen if I didn't settle the situation immediately. I had fallen behind. My life was spinning out of control. It had been that kind of summer. It was the summer the debt rating of the United States itself had been slashed. We were a nation of deadbeats.

The stranger agreed that Bethel Woods was transcendent and that kicking the tour off there was an inspired choice.

We sat down on the floor of the Greyhound station next to a pair of scraggly-haired, hard-living denizens who had the grizzled look endemic to the native Ohio Juggalo.

It was this curious book in microcosm: a strange summit of the tribes, between a Phish fan, a pair of defiant Juggalos, and a strange man with scratched glasses and a black eye that took up half his face at a Greyhound bus station in weird, gothic, massive, endless Ohio.

"Man, whenever I go back to jail they know I'm a Juggalo just by this tattoo," one of the Juggalos boasted as he pulled down his T-shirt to reveal a backward Hatchetman. "I got this backward Hatchetman for my dead friend who was killed by Juggalo Holocaust. I told him if the fuckers ever got him, I'd get a backward Hatchetman in his memory. They did, so it is what it is."

They were both high-ranking leaders within a gang they called the Hatchets that may or may not have existed solely in their

active imaginations. The gang was consequently clashing with
factions of an actual anti-ICP group called Juggalo Holocaust.
According to the men, Juggalos were being slaughtered en masse
by rival gangs. They told tales, chockablock with Juggalo bravado,
of being approached by Juggalo Holocaust thugs and letting out a
"Whoop! Whoop!" to signal to their boys that it was about to pop
off, of losing friends to gang fights, and buying *The Great Milenko*
at age seven and being instantly transformed into Juggalos.

It soon became apparent, however, that the men did not
entirely seem to know what numbers meant. They had boasted
that the Gathering attracts 3.2 million people every year, which
would be impossible even if it somehow occupied most of a major
city, let alone a tiny little circle of nowhere called Cave-in-Rock.

The two men were in a furious race to determine who could
relate the most sordid anecdotes in the least time. There was a distinct element of gamesmanship to it; one of the Juggalos talked
about getting stabbed; the other copped to getting shot in the leg
while innocently waving a gun at the person who shot him.

"I was in fucking hell, prison for eleven months, man. And
I did it all for love. My fucking 'lette, man. She's my goddamn
heart. My life would be so much easier if I could just fucking let
it go and move on but I can't. The last time I saw my PO he even
said to me, 'You still love her, don't you?' and I was all, 'Shit.
Yeah,'" the Juggalo with the scraggly beard said with unexpected
tenderness. When he spoke of his 'lette his bravado faded a little
to reveal an incongruous vulnerability.

It was disarming until the bearded man mentioned that he
was six years older than the woman he ended up in jail for fuck-

ing (with her parents' consent, he was quick to point out) and that at fifteen, she would be legal in just three years. I started to do the math, then stopped abruptly when it got too ugly.

"I don't fucking know my family, man. My family fucking hates me. This is my family. Juggalos are my family. Both our dads are Hell's Angels and they fucking hate Juggalos. Everybody hates Juggalos. The girl I got in trouble for, she's fucking dating a Juggalo Holocaust now," the hirsute Juggalo lamented.

"Shit, if he's dating a real 'lette then he ain't no real Juggalo Holocaust," the man's friend added.

"Sometimes, man, I miss her so fucking much, I miss her so fucking much," he began, "that I'll just call her phone over and over again from other people's phones and other people's houses just so I can hear her voice for just a few seconds. It's enough for me just to hear her say hello."

The man smiled, but it was a sad smile.

The topic then switched to topics more conventionally associated with Juggalos. A snitch had infiltrated their gang, they announced dramatically, before speculating about his identity.

It felt as if they were putting on a show for us, but it wasn't until the conversation nose-dived into unsavory territory that the Phish fan got a little wary. He had never heard of Juggalos or Insane Clown Posse, but he had the kind of open mind that wants and needs to believe the best about people. Billy, the Phish fan, didn't judge. He was hungry for experience, but he didn't judge.

Billy was bursting with excitement and curiosity about the world around him. Greyhound buses are a little like Phish shows:

You don't necessarily have to go around making introductions or asking questions because people are all too happy to talk. If you're as shy and self-conscious as I am, that's enormous comfort.

I'm not particularly sure how the exchange began, but the man seated behind Billy and me decided to fill the dead time between cities with an elaborate monologue about his life. Once upon a time he was a big-time college football star. "Big-time," he told us. "Look me up." Those were the glory years. "Girls were into the whole football thing, being with a big football-playing stud." Then college ended, and with it his ephemeral sports fame. He was no longer the star attraction anymore. As the roar of the crowd faded and then dissipated entirely, he began drinking more and more.

The man kept stressing how important he had been, how people had looked up to him. He'd had girls, plenty of them. Then he'd slipped into an endless personal freefall that showed no signs of ending or even slowing down.

He was headed to Cincinnati, he declared, to handle some important business. He was going to find his wife and win her back, he proclaimed. She had taken up with another man. He was no good for her. He beat her. So he was going to either win his wife back or get drunker and go searching for pussy. As with the Juggalos, there was an undeniable element of performance to the man's monologue. At one point the man had an animated conversation on his phone that Billy suspected, not without cause, he was staging exclusively for our benefit.

Hunger continued to elude me. It was conspicuous in its absence. In my state I could only fantasize about what it would be like to want to eat. That was the curious condition I found myself in: I wanted to want. I hungered to hunger. Yet my stomach decided that it was no longer in the food-eating business. Like the rest of me, it didn't seem to know what to do. It had turned against me.

Yet in a cruel burlesque, Billy and I traveled to a Big Boy in Cincinnati all the same. Billy had the gaunt, wired look of someone who has never eaten and perhaps never will. I looked at food with palpable revulsion. We were quite the duo, a pair of roadworn lunatics engaging in the preposterous masquerade that we were interested in a primal human endeavor like eating.

Our waiter was mentally challenged, and when Billy asked about the salad dressings you could see the furious mental exertion at play as he strived to remember every option. There was something quietly heroic about the man's understated professionalism, a poignant quality to his striving. It was a lot of work to remember all those dressings, but he was up to it. Billy is a talker, and when he talked to the waiter I couldn't quite ascertain whether he was sizing him up, fucking with him, or genuinely trying to engage with him. That was the live-wire duality of Billy.

Travel enhances. If I'd never dropped acid in the bathroom at that Big Boy in Cincinnati and conversed with the waiter, for example, I never would have learned that in Big Boys west of Ohio, the restaurant chain's signature hamburger is served with Thousand Island as its "special sauce," while east of Ohio, tartar sauce is the flavoring of choice. For some reason this information felt enormously important to me at the time. In hindsight, it may have been the acid.

If I had any questions as to where Billy was coming from when he bantered with our waiter, they were answered when he faced the waiter's boss, shook his hand, and told him, "I just wanted to tell you that our waiter did the best job of any waiter I've ever had. I just thought you should know that."

Anticipating the comment, the manager responded, "You know what, sir? We have someone say just about the same thing during every single one of his shifts."

I was lost and far from home the summer of 2011, but Phish's carnival of light was like a beacon leading home, emotionally if not geographically. As exhilaratingly foreign as the road could be, especially when it's traversed via long, sleepless Greyhound bus rides, there was something extraordinarily comforting about the Lot, about seeing the same vendors and T-shirt stands and gloriously alive, wonderfully unselfconscious people in venue after venue.

I loved hanging around the Lot with Billy. For someone who had squeezed an awful lot of living into his twenty-four years, a lot of it hard, some of it agonizingly painful (nearly a year in prison, a stint dealing drugs), he still retained a remarkable capacity for joy and wonder. He looked at the homemade T-shirts with winking Phish in-jokes and handmade posters and delicious-smelling but stomach-twisting and suspiciously cheap foodstuffs with amused appreciation and nothing in the way of cynicism. He said that someday he wanted his children to be the doe-eyed waifs selling dollar waters after a show. I wanted my children to go to Phish shows as well, albeit in less of a child-labor-intensive capacity, though given the dire financial straits

I now found myself in it might not hurt the theoretical future children of mine to brush up on their water-selling skills.

We sat in the woods near a ring of nitrous oxide tanks and talked to a woman in her thirties who spoke about how she had followed Phish for a summer while pregnant. She had experienced a natural high dancing sober with a baby in her womb. We talked to a guy and his buddy passing a bottle of whiskey back and forth about the differences between Phish and Furthur and the Disco Biscuits and Widespread Panic shows.

By that point the Lot felt strangely like home and the songs like old friends. Sometimes that's because I'd lived with them for decades, like the killer version of the Talking Heads' "Crosseyed and Painless" that anchored the band's second set that night in Cincinnati or the Rolling Stones' "Loving Cup" from *Exile on Main Street,* one of those albums that had the respectable critics' stamp of approval.

Once upon a time I had a knee-jerk aversion to Phish playing funk. Like so many of my first impressions regarding Phish and their fans, that now seems incredibly close-minded of me. Phish are phenomenal at playing funk. It doesn't matter that they're pasty middle-aged white men.

It was stupid of me to feel otherwise. On good nights, Page plays the synthesizers and keyboards like the second coming of Bernie Worrell, Trey plays a mean funk guitar, and Mike and Fishman form a ferociously tight rhythm section, the cornerstone of every good funk outfit.

It was dumb of me to think Phish performing a Stevie Wonder song called "Boogie On Reggae Woman" was ridiculous because, c'mon, they're a bunch of assistant-professor-looking mother-fuckers and the song is called "Boogie On Reggae Woman." Now I wish they played it every concert. Hell, I wish they played it for me every morning when I wake up. There's something incredibly liberating about that cover and Phish's gloriously unselfconscious embrace of funk in general.

Speaking of friends and dancing white boys, I looked behind me during Phish's second set that night and saw the Golden Child and Kevin Corrigan's doppelgänger dancing shirtless and deliri-ous. I wanted to go over and say hi, but I was caught up in the moment and when I looked behind me again a song or two later they were gone. It was like they were apparitions or mirages. One moment they were there, the next they weren't.

While I was free to continue my strange voyage, Billy took a night Greyhound to Buffalo to return to a job he felt ambiva-lent about at best. So I said good-bye to him after the Cincinnati show as he boarded a bus back to his hometown with a mind full of trepidation and a body racked with something like ten hits of acid. Billy was due back at work imminently, but I had a night or two before the next show. I mentioned to Billy that I would be looking for some weed to help me sleep through the night when I shuffled up to Buffalo later myself.

Billy booked me into a Motel 6 he had a long and compli-cated history with and waited for me to hit town. Immediately upon returning to Buffalo, he had tried to give a homeless man at the bus station twenty bucks and got robbed of his entire wal-let in the process. That was Billy in a nutshell: He possessed the kind of ferocious, indiscriminate, and reckless kindness that can get you in trouble. Scratch that. He possessed the kind of ferocious, indiscriminate, and reckless kindness that *will* get you in trouble. There were no half measures in his world: Everything was done with pummeling intensity and absolute conviction.

When I finally arrived at the Motel 6 in Buffalo late the night of June 7, Billy and his best friend, Matthew, were waiting for me with a look of impish delight. Billy told me that in his drug-dealing days he'd made that particular Motel 6 his home base. His eyes danced as he recounted half-forgotten ragers, bottles of coke, oceans of meth, and enough K to wipe out a small continent. His stories made me feel a dark, malevolent energy to the Motel 6. It felt absolutely nothing like Tom Bodett had made it out to be. I'm pretty sure they hadn't left the lights on for us.

Though he could be quiet and introverted at times, when he was feeling chatty, Billy always talked more than was necessary. He talked because he had bottomless curiosity about the world but also because he liked to fuck with people. He may not have been a con artist, but he had a con artist's intuitive grasp of human nature, the preternatural ability to read people instantly, and the gift of gab.

So by the time I checked into the Motel 6, Billy had chatted up some old connection and when we headed up to my room things got sordid very quickly. All I wanted was enough weed to last me through the night, but as soon as Billy, Matthew, and I passed the threshold, my hotel room stopped being my phenomenally shitty hotel room and became a drug den.

"Do you mind if we bump some K here in your room?" Matthew asked eagerly.

I confess that I had no idea what he was talking about and misheard his question as, "Do you mind if I bottle some keys?"

I didn't want to be rude so I said sure, at which point he began chopping up queasy-looking lines of powder the color and consistency of laundry detergent and started snorting. There were deep black bags under Matthew's eyes. His eyes looked glassy and lost. He was a nice kid, but he was gone into the ether.

Every element of the scenario amplified the sadness: The dinginess of the hotel room was exacerbated by the overpowering stench of smoke, failure, and desperation. The incongruously chipper bedspread seemed to make a mockery of a bed that barely qualified as a double. Billy and Matthew were lost in their own little world, snorting lines of what I later found out was ketamine and trading stories that meandered and meandered en route to going nowhere.

"Do you mind if I smoke?" Matthew asked.

"Go right ahead."

"No. I mean, I understand completely if you don't want me to smoke in your room. It's not a big deal. I could just as easily go outside and smoke," Matthew replied empathetically.

"Dude. You're doing lines in my hotel room. It's okay if you smoke."

I was at best a day tripper, a Sunday driver, yeah. All it took was some lines of K and the lost look in my new friends' eyes to make me feel terribly melancholy. I wasn't surprised, just sad, though that sadness and the judgment it implied felt awfully hypocritical considering the mind-altering substances I'd already consumed during the journey and the fact that I had specifically asked them for drugs.

Throughout the evening, friends of Billy and Matthew's passed in and out of the doors of my sad little motel room to do lines, smoke pot, and bask in the majestic beauty that is the Buffalo Motel 6. Eventually the young mob disappeared and I was able to sleep and prepare myself for Billy's big hometown show in Darien Lake. As if all that wasn't exciting enough, the Darien Lake show included a free pass to the water park connected to the venue.

Phish! Water slides! Wave pools! Pirate-themed attractions!

My new friends did not quite feel the same way. Being locals, the water park didn't hold the same exotic appeal for them that it did for me. When we got to the venue they loitered around the Lot, taking in the sights, sounds, and smells while my interior monologue/inner child impatiently pleaded, "Water park! Water park! Water park! Water park! Let's all go the water park! There are slides and rides and attractions of all kinds! Let's all regress in a hippie-friendly environment!" I wanted to see what a theme park populated exclusively by Phish fans would look like. I wanted to experience the hippie takeover of a wholesome family institution. As with Insane Clown Posse and the Gathering of the Juggalos, there was something incongruously innocent and childlike at the core of the debauched circus that was a Phish tour, and nothing spoke to this duality more strongly than the prospect of an afternoon at a water park and then an evening of drugged-up exhilaration at a show.

It was to no avail. After failing to convince my friends, I ended up trekking over to the water park by myself, and while I tried to make the most of it, there are few things in the world sadder than a solitary thirty-five-year-old man on an inner tube in a wave pool surrounded by families and toked-up revelers partying with their friends.

After about an hour, I headed back to the Lot to hang out with Billy and his friends. They were sitting peacefully in a circle underneath a giant tree.

I enjoyed the Darien Lake show just as I had enjoyed every Phish show, but there was something unmistakably melancholy about it. My time on the road was drawing to a close. I was torn between this exhilarating path and the ferocious pull of home, both in the form of a woman I loved and missed with every fiber of my being and a job that was much more to me than a job.

In the second set Phish played "Backwards Down the Number Line," the opening track on 2009's *Joy*, the comeback studio album after Anastasio's arrest and the crumbling of the Phish empire. It is both my favorite Phish song and a song that eloquently seemed to capture everything that I was feeling that summer, all the joy and sadness and regret and hope and feverish nostalgia for a past I had never experienced firsthand but foolishly sought to recapture for myself.

Maybe that's what we're all looking for: art that reflects who we are, what we've been through, and how we see the world; art as a deep, dark, truthful mirror. It's poetically apt that an album heralding a fresh start for Phish begins by invoking the past in such a heartbreakingly bittersweet way.

According to Anastasio's introduction when he debuted the song at the Rothbury Folk Festival with Gordon on bass in 2008, his songwriting partner Tom Marshall sent him the lyrics on his birthday in 2007. The two were estranged at the time, or at least were not collaborating, but Anastasio was so moved by the words that he translated them to music and their fruitful and fortuitous partnership was reignited. At the Rothbury festival, Anastasio says he thinks it's about "getting younger," but like so much of Phish's music, it's open to interpretation: It means exactly what you want it to mean.

To me, it's a birthday song about the fundamentally bittersweet nature of birthdays, how we at once celebrate surviving another year while simultaneously hurtling closer to the grave, away from the sanctity and promise of a youth we can mourn and romanticize but never regain. But it's also a song about the complicated nature of partnerships, about how the inexorable march of time and a shared history can both pull us together and tear us apart. I loved the way that Trey's voice strained poignantly to hit the notes that night, especially at the beginning, how its delicacy renders it forever just out of his vocal reach but he makes a heroic effort all the same. I love how human and vulnerable and aching the song sounds. I love the words, but the words wouldn't mean anywhere near as much as they do, and the song wouldn't be anywhere near as profound, without all the complicated history behind it, not just between Trey and the band but also the band and its fans, the fans and one another, and Trey and Tom Marshall. To paraphrase Tippy Walker's character in *The World of Henry Orient*—a film, appropriately enough, about rabid musical fandom—hearing "Backwards Down the Number Line" made me awfully happy in a sort of sad way.

After the show, Billy, Matthew, some of their friends, and I

picked up a ride home from a Phish fan who ran in the same
circles as my new friends. Alas, they had partied just a little too
hard and taken too much acid and questioned whether they were
up to the task at hand.

"I cannot drive in the condition I'm in. I better go over to
the Lot and score me some coke so I can sober up for the road
in case there's a roadblock," the driver reasoned with exquisitely
stoned counterlogic.

His pupils were the size of dimes. Dreadlocks hung down
from his fitted baseball cap. He was exiting a Phish Lot. A bum-
per sticker reading, DEAR POLICE: PLEASE SEARCH MY VEHICLE
FOR ILLEGAL DRUGS BECAUSE I HAVE A FUCK-TON would have
been exquisitely redundant since everything in the man's manner, clothes, hair, and bearing conveyed the same sentiment
more succinctly.

Everyone in the Lot sent out a similar message. The "police"
presence in the Lot took on a farcical element. At the car next
to us, a shirtless, cargo-shorts-clad man was so wasted he forgot where he put his keys and had cops rifle through his pockets to retrieve them, which they inexplicably did. At the same
time, there was a certain safety in numbers: As at seemingly
every Phish show, the prevailing philosophy among the stoned
seemed to be, They can't arrest all of us, so hopefully they won't
bother arresting any of us, or at the very least refrain from arresting me personally.

We rambled back to the Lot and bided our time nervously
while our ride tried to sober up.

As we drove to the house Billy shared with his family, the dreadlocked driver put some electronic music on the stereo. "Aw man. I went to one of their shows and fell in love. It's been on ever since."

He was, of course, talking about the Disco Biscuits. They were Matthew's favorite band. He'd literally gone to hundreds of Biscuits shows but only about fifteen or sixteen Phish shows.

As someone who grew up in a group home and a series of crappy apartments, I stand in awe of the fully appointed suburban family home. To me it is a thing of infinite wonder and majesty, and Billy's family had a beauty. It had everything: a basement den with a television and a giant bed, an outdoor pool, and, most spectacularly, a veranda that transformed the backyard of a suburban Buffalo residence into a quaint little Parisian outdoor salon circa 1923.

The house could have been in *The Graduate*. It was a house with history, with stories. Billy spoke excitedly of his older brother, who had introduced him to the whole scene when he got into the Grateful Dead as a teenager. He was never that into drugs; he just smoked a little weed and drank and listened to the music, but he'd done an about-face as of late, straightened up his act, and gone the MBA J.Crew route.

Billy wasn't exaggerating. His brother was straight out of the *Preppy Handbook*. There was pain in his eyes as well. It was a look I recognized in each of Billy's family members when they looked at him: love mixed with pain and concern.

Billy talked about his brothers all the time. He was blessed and cursed with an exceptional family. They loved each other. The roots were deep. The Grateful Dead was a tradition each brother passed down to the other.

It was all wrapped up in one: the good and the bad, the joy
and the pain. Turning Billy on to the Dead meant introducing
him to an exhilarating new world of music and people and ideas
and energy. But it also meant starting him down a path that
would eventually lead to prison. I experienced profoundly mixed
feelings when Billy said he'd bought some deemster (the street
name for the drug dimethyltryptamine, or DMT) to smoke with
his younger brother.

DMT was some serious shit, a total fucking godhead next-
level psychedelic mind-bender. The Disco Biscuits fans who had
sold it to him said it contained a chemical that otherwise exists
only in the human mind in the moments immediately before
death. I was not going to fuck with DMT in the frame of mind
I was in. I had rolled the dice with my fragile mental health
before, when I took acid the first night at Bethel. I didn't want to
push my luck. Who knew what kind of darkness lay within my
psyche? I had demons I did not want to conjure up. I didn't want
to confront the messes I had made. I was half convinced I was
beyond redemption. Nothing terrified me more than the truth.

At Billy's family home we were joined by an angel-faced boy
with a dodgy reputation and his girlfriend, a smart, tough survivor who conveyed a steeliness and sense of determination
beyond her young years.

At one point in the evening everyone else had nodded off in
their chairs and the only ones still awake were Matthew and me.
Matthew continued to read the Wikipedia entry on different
kinds of nitrous gas in a borderline hypnotic monotone. I'm not
entirely sure he was aware he was talking out loud; as with the

man on the bus, it felt like I was privy to someone else's interior monologue.

He was a sweet kid but he had staked his entire life on being the guy in the Lot who'll hook you up with a ticket and help you get fucked up. In the parlance of my people, he was a consummate mensch, but for him a mitzvah involved scoring some Special K or a roll of acid.

Like many of the people I encountered over the course of my travels, he viewed the festival and Phish scene in ways that bordered on animistic; it was all about honoring the spirit of the music and engendering good karma. If you gave out love, you would receive it back sevenfold. So he habitually went to shows without a ticket, trusting that the spirit of the shows would not let him down. By his recounting, it never did.

He told me stories that after a while faded into one long, complicated list of mood-altering substances. Here's the thing about drug stories: They don't make sense and they're not interesting to anybody except the people involved. (Yes, I realize how deeply that statement incriminates me and this entire book.) Yet people who use drugs feel the need to tell them all the same, like a form of contemporary folklore.

Some of the drug stories inevitably involved the sale of bogus drugs on the Lot; for a head, that was a major transgression. "It's bad enough that we take drugs, but then you gotta have people making you feel even dirtier for it 'cause they're ripping you off," Matthew said sadly.

We had all been told that drugs were bad. They changed you. They corrupted you. They turned you into somebody you didn't know and didn't like. They alienated you from your friends and families. They cost you your job and your freedom. Yet we took them anyway and tried not to let our consciences keep us up at night.

The ugliness was never far from the surface. The angel-faced kid had a reputation. He had burned people. He had ripped people off. He had lied to people and hurt friends because he cared more about drugs than he did about people. Being a drug person involves being friends with people you don't like or trust because you share the same weakness. A drug friend is only a friend as long as drugs are around; if things go awry, they can quickly morph into drug enemies.

With drugs, everything can turn on a dime; let the moment linger too long and a hazy narcotic paradise has a curious way of darkening. Billy's friends had already reached that point. They'd passed it.

"I don't like the person my friend has become since she got really into drugs," the angel-faced stoner's girlfriend said of one of her other druggie friends. She was too smart and too practical to continue making the same mistakes much longer. She looked over at her boyfriend with regret. There was a lot of ugly history there that it's probably best I didn't know about.

I looked at a picture of Billy and his ex-fiancée. They looked so goddamn innocent, like the kids they were. "I really love her. That's my ex-fiancée and it didn't work out, but I still think of her all the time—she's in my heart, man," Billy said when I looked at the picture.

I wanted more than anything to find Billy a nice girl. I wanted to find him a Cadence. I wanted him to find somebody who would tell him to slow down and eat and sleep and take his time and not be in such a goddamn hurry to get wherever the fuck it was he seemed to be speeding two hundred miles an hour toward without brakes.

I worried about him. Everyone else did as well. They were right to. Deep into the night Billy's father came home and told us all to leave immediately. He cast us out over Billy's strenuous objections and apologies.

What I saw on the man's face was not rage but pain. It was pain mixed with love. It was an old pain, an ancient hurt from a culture war that began long ago and never stops raging. It was the old hurt of parents terrified that this strange music and these unsavory characters are going to take their children away from them. It was the pain of parents dreading inevitable phone calls from the cops that their son or daughter has been arrested or killed. It's the pain of not being able to understand the music and the culture that has taken over your child's life and the sadness and rage and confusion that come with trying to acclimate yourself to a world whose rules and codes of conduct are incomprehensible.

Some part of me wanted to embrace the man, to tell him that I was with him, that even though I'd only met his son a few days ago I was already unhealthily invested in his happiness. I wanted to save him because I didn't think I was capable of saving myself.

"I'm only twenty-four and I'm already tired," Billy said without needing to. The exhaustion on his face said it all.

He had seen too much on the road. They all had. He had seen

things he should never have seen. He'd been to prison. He'd been a drug dealer. He'd been a shark. He'd seen money come. He'd seen money go. I thought about the girl behind me on the night-time Greyhound bus who said that at twenty she was finally ready to settle down, even if it was only with herself.

It struck me as ridiculous at the time, but now I could see how people could feel they had experienced all of the excitement and adventure they ever need for a lifetime before hitting their midtwenties.

Darien Lake was Billy's hometown show, so it had special resonance for him. To mark the occasion, I bought him a print in the Lot and felt for the first time in a very long while like a half-way decent human being. Perhaps that's what this journey was about in the first place: the journey to make a friend. Singular or plural. To get out of the prison of my mind and genuinely connect with another human being, if only for a little while.

THE WALKING WOUNDED:
COMING HOME

Billy returned to the workaday world after Darien Lake, leaving me to go it alone to Phish's next stop in Camden, New Jersey. By that point homesickness had kicked in hard. I missed Cadence fiercely. I missed the curve of her lips, the softness of her hair, the contours of her body. I missed the way she smelled. I missed the way she talked, her wit, her flair for drama. In a thousand lifetimes it would never have occurred to me to go see Phish, let alone write a book about them, if Cadence hadn't turned my life upside down and reintroduced me to the concept of joy. Damn you, Cadence! You can't miss something you've never experienced, and now I felt as if I had driven myself half insane chasing joy through Greyhound bus stations and outdoor arenas and parking lots.

I didn't talk to Cadence much from the road. How could I? I struggled to put into words what I was feeling and doing and experiencing.

I wasn't sure I understood what was happening to my mind and my body and I feared I wouldn't be able to explain it to anyone else, even someone who felt like a part of me, even someone I felt connected to at the soul. I experienced everything intensely that summer. Everything made me cry. Loudon Wainwright III's music devastated me with its elegiac meditation on worlds lost to time. I wept openly because I was sad. I wept openly because I felt joy. I wept openly because I didn't understand what was happening to me. I couldn't quite tell if I liked the person I was becoming or not, but I felt as if I was undeniably changing.

Cadence interpreted my radio silence from the road through a much darker filter. She thought I was planning to break up with her as soon as I returned. The truth of the matter was that I had made a huge decision regarding the future of our relationship, but it wasn't at all what Cadence had feared.

From Buffalo I took a Greyhound to Penn Station in New York and then a train from Penn Station to Philadelphia, where I called Cadence from an Amtrak train and she uttered words that filled me with terror and foreboding.

"I can move my stuff out of the condo by Monday if you'd like," she told me with an air of weary resignation.

"No! No!" I screamed out loud to the evident mortification of the perfectly respectable folks seated next to me on the train.

"Really? Because that's what you seem to want."

Panic overtook me. I felt out of control. I felt powerless. I wanted to stop the train and get off and regain my composure, but I was hardwired to my seat. With mounting desperation in my voice, I begged Cadence not to leave. I tried to explain that the last thing that I wanted was for her to move out of the place I'd bought specifically to provide a home worthy of her. I wanted to explain to her that she was the reason I was on the road, she was the reason I was writing this book, that she was the reason I was on this journey. But words failed me. Words were all I had, and words were suddenly hopelessly inadequate. The longer we talked, the more distraught I became. Everything felt like it was spiraling out of control, and all I had was my clunky suitcase and a plan that made less sense by the day. I wanted to continue down this road, but everything seemed to be calling me back to Chicago, to my office and cubicle and home and family and soul mate.

By the time the train chugged into the station in Philadelphia and a cabdriver took me to the Sheraton University City Hotel, I was running on empty. The elation of early shows had morphed into an unmistakable weariness, and while I still eagerly anticipated each show, I would be lying if I didn't concede that there was part of me that deeply resented the way Phish kept forcing their fans to travel long distances to get to New Jersey. It seemed unspeakably cruel.

We finally reached the Susquehanna Bank Center, and I passed a man shouting hoarsely into his iPhone in a thick New Jersey accent, "I swear to God, I spent a hundred and seventy-five dollars on this girl. Dinner, tickets, parking, everything, and I don't get nothing from her. Not a blow job, no sex, no nothing. So I'm angry, of course, and it's like, what a fucking waste!"

When it came to towns in New Jersey, Camden was no Holmdel. I experienced a surge of excitement when Phish opened with "Rocky Top," a bluegrass standard I had once seen Bobby Osborne and the Rocky Top X-Press perform at the Grand Ole Opry. "Rocky Top" is one of Tennessee's eight official state songs, which suggests the state is both enthusiastic to a fault and has a lot of difficulty making up its goddamn mind. I wanted to concentrate on the concert, but my conversation with Cadence that afternoon had spooked me something awful. Both personally and professionally I had left behind a hell of a mess in Chicago before I left, and I had no idea what awaited me when I returned home.

I just knew that I couldn't stand to be apart from Cadence any longer, and I wanted to make sure I still had a job to come home to. I feared that any more time on the road might imperil that possibility.

So while the Sheraton was lovely and the Camden show was dynamic and exciting enough to make me forget that I was in New Jersey for a few idyllic hours, I decided afterward that, on the whole, I would rather not be in Philadelphia, so I booked a flight and flew home to Chicago the next day.

I had only been on the road for two weeks, yet I returned home a new man, much worse for wear but nowhere near as emotionally apocalyptic as I'd been when I set out on a dark and scary road just a few weeks earlier.

I looked the way I felt: broken and battered. At six foot two, I was down to 160 pounds. A purple-pink scar now adorned my left eyebrow. I was weary and shattered and in dire need of Cadence. The kindness-seeking missile had returned home.

But not for long! Phish's annual festival Super Ball X loomed tantalizingly in our near future. I had abused my body and myself throughout my Phish tour as only a single man with no regard for his health, safety, sanity, or survival truly could, but now my solo misadventures were over and I could once again experience Phish with the woman who had inspired this whole glorious, maddening endeavor.

By the time I returned home from tour, my relationship with Phish was radically different. The connection I felt to the band, its music, its fans, and its scene was no longer vicarious. It was no longer a by-product of the intense love I felt toward Cadence. No, my Phish fandom now had a curious, traumatic, and joyous history all its own.

A few weeks after I came back from the road, I saw my psychiatrist for the first time in several months.

When I talked about the road with my psychiatrist, it almost felt as if I were talking about another person. I talked about how I felt like my center of balance was off and I could topple at any moment, how my mind raced with thoughts, how a thick fog of dread had descended upon me before I headed out on tour and convinced me I would not make it past October, that I would be destroyed somewhere along the way. I talked about how food had lost its appeal for me on the road, how even foods I'd once loved tasted like ash in my mouth.

I talked about how I fantasized not about specific foods but about the very concept of hunger. I talked about my LSD epiphany the first night in Bethel and how in some strange way it and the community of Phish fans seemed to have saved me from myself, how I'd get dizzy and lose track of where I was and who I was and feel like I was about to be hurtled into an all-encompassing abyss.

As I spoke, my psychiatrist got a purposeful look on her face that concerned me. Something was wrong with me. Something was desperately wrong with me on the road, but I didn't know what it was. That ignorance was simultaneously terrifying and exhilarating. I am not immune to the tawdry, self-mythologizing romance of depression and mental illness. It's one of the few perks of being a crazy person.

"I think that it sounds like," my psychiatrist began brightly, "judging from your experiences on the road, that you might have a mild case of"—she paused dramatically, or at least it felt that way to me—"bipolar disorder."

The "bipolar disorder" part of that equation completely negated the "mild" part. My first response was denial. I couldn't be a manic-depressive. Where were the manic episodes? Where was the mind racing and thoughts jumbling madly and talking up a storm and writing, writing, writing as if my heart would stop beating the moment I stopped? Oh yeah. That's what I had been experiencing for the past few months. At first I thought it might be panic attacks, but the more I thought about it, the more my shrink's diagnosis made sense.

When I told people later of the bipolar diagnosis, nobody seemed the least bit surprised. No one muttered, "That can't be right! Not you! You seem so sane and grounded!" Instead the responses I received were more of the "Well, duh!" and "What took them so long to figure that shit out?" variety.

Whatever I had, my friend Billy had it too. I thought about sitting with him at that Big Boy in Kentucky with two profoundly unappetizing meals we both knew neither of us was going to eat. I thought about him sitting silently in a stoned, seemingly semicomatose state in the gazebo that night at his family home before suddenly jutting upright and talking a blue streak about everything and anything, the words spilling out of his mouth in an uncontrollable burst.

Now I was able to put a name to that unsettling and oddly intoxicating feeling I'd been experiencing for the past few months: bipolar disorder. I was bipolar, which felt like both a cause for relief and a cause for concern.

When I mentioned the bipolar diagnosis to my therapist (I'm one of those lucky souls who gets to see both a therapist and a psychiatrist) later, she said her colleagues joked that there were primarily two kinds of bipolar disorder. There was the kind that got you promoted and the kind that got you arrested. I was pretty sure I had the first kind. I feared that unless it was treated, it would morph into the second variety. The diagnosis lent clarity to emotions I'd been experiencing over the course of the tour even if it felt a little fuzzy.

Am I bipolar? I honestly don't know. I suspect my psychiatrist doesn't ultimately know either. She's subsequently conceded that she doesn't know exactly what happened to me that summer, whether my seeming mental break was attributable to bipolar disorder, the drugs I was on—prescription and otherwise—or the pressure I was under. At the time, my diagnosis felt like an answer I didn't even realize I was looking for, but I suspect I will never truly know exactly what happened to my mind during the summer of 2011: It remains a mystery, even to myself. But if the ultimate cause of my breakdown remains unknown, the bipolar medication (the powerful sedative and antipsychotic Seroquel) my psychiatrist prescribed did wonders for my mood and sanity, so I approached the arrival of Phish's massive Super Ball festival in upstate New York feeling saner and steadier than I had for a very, very long time.

BACK IN A NEW YORK GROOVE: FEELING LIKE A KARMA BILLIONAIRE AT SUPER BALL 2011

When I first saw Phish in Miami during their New Year's Eve run in 2009, it meant little to me. When I went with Cadence to see Phish play their annual festival Super Ball IX in Watkins Glen, New York, in July 2011, it meant everything. Whatever outsider credentials I might have possessed were gone, replaced with the guileless enthusiasm of a zealot.

I didn't just want to see Phish; I needed to see them. Wild horses couldn't keep me away from Watkins Glen, where I would be experiencing my very first one-band festival. You know who plays at Super Ball IX? Fucking Phish. You know who else? Nobody. If Phish were any other band, this might come off as the height of arrogance. After all, it's one thing to see Phish perform for four hours over the course of a single night. But an entire weekend of four-hour Phish sets? That registered as unbelievable generosity, an unimaginable abundance of riches.

The festival took place at the Watkins Glen Grand Prix Raceway, a gloriously natural venue that in 1973 hosted the single largest festival in rock history to date, the Summer Jam featuring the Allman Brothers, the Band, and, naturally enough, the Grateful Dead.

If left to my own devices, I would happily settle for a low-budget realm of Greyhounds and Motel 6's, but I wanted better for Cadence, so we signed up for a package deal for Super Ball IX that included everything: tickets to the festival, lodgings at a nearby Ramada, and buses to and from the show every day and night. It was a little like going to summer camp in your mid-thirties, only with drugs and Phish and no responsible authority figures to ruin your fun. In that respect it was like the most funnest summer camp ever.

The excitement on July 1, the first day of Super Ball IX, was infectious and irresistible, a replay of the feverish anticipation that preceded the monumental first show of the tour at Bethel Woods, a soul-consuming sense of exhilaration at the prospect of three whole days of nothing but Phish. For a brief idyll, Watkins

Glen turned into a city exclusively for Phish fans. It was a jam-band utopia, an entire world that springs to life for a few days every year, then goes into hibernation until it's time for the next Super Ball to come around.

Super Ball IX was a little like a Phish tour in microcosm. It begins with boundless excitement and anticipation, with a spirit of optimism so thick you can feel it in the air, and ends with the audience feeling simultaneously exhausted and exhilarated.

For all the open drug use on display, there was something unmistakably wholesome about the whole affair. Maybe it was the Ferris wheel towering high over the fairgrounds at Watkins Glen, or the preponderance of booths for do-gooder organizations such as Phish's pet charity, the WaterWheel Foundation, but it was remarkably wholesome for a Phish festival and a far cry, thank God, from the bad vibes of Coventry.

More than anything, Super Ball IX had time on its side, something Trey underlined when, after an appropriately epic "Bathtub Gin," he casually remarked, "We're not in any rush because we're going to be here for, like, four days or something," to the rapturous applause of the crowd. Accordingly, the group's first set of the festival was even more relaxed and unhurried than usual, with soulful covers of David Bowie's "Life on Mars"; "Peaches En Regalia," by my guardian angel from the first night at Bethel, Frank Zappa; an exquisitely exhausted, world-weary, and rare version of "Torn and Frayed" from the Rolling Stones' *Exile on Main Street*; Ween's "Roses Are Free"; and Bob Dylan's "Quinn the Eskimo," along with inspired renditions of originals like the set-opening "Possum," "The Wolfman's Brother," and "Bathtub

Gin." Playing the first set of a three-day festival, Phish had nothing but time on their hands, and they made the most of it.

The pleasant-Friday-in-the-country vibe underlined the reassuring truth that there was absolutely nothing cool about Phish in 2011. They had become a quintessential geek fixation in that they appealed almost exclusively to a small but fiercely committed subsection of the populace that was knowledgeable and invested in the group to an almost unhealthy degree; they meant nothing to the vast majority of the population. Three decades on, Phish fans could still believe, with justification, that the band was still their own special thing, that it belonged to them and not to the world at large. There is a beauty and a purity that comes with never making it into the mainstream, with never quite breaking through, either by design or happenstance.

Like the Gathering of the Juggalos, Super Ball IX drew the geekiest of the geeks, the hardest of the hardcore. Phish shows may have a richly merited reputation as good places to score and use drugs, but no one was going to make the trek all the way to Watkins Glen, New York, and listen to one band perform for nearly eleven hours over the course of three days solely to score some Molly, just as the remoteness of Cave-in-Rock seemed designed to scare away neophytes and dilettantes attracted by the infamy of the Gathering.

So it seemed altogether appropriate that upon entering the festival, we sat by a picnic table where we uncovered a familiar novelty: the contemporary Juggalo, far outside his natural habitat. The two Juggalos were recognizable by their telltale markings: The stouter of the two sported a Hatchetman with a cane, while the thinner Juggalo sported one of the Amazing Jeckel brothers on each of his legs.

Cadence always gets excited when we spy Juggalos, especially in such a seemingly incongruous context. But if this treatise has taught us anything, it's that seemingly impregnable divides are nowhere near as concrete as they appear, and unbridgeable gulfs have a strange way of proving strangely bridgeable.

"Are y'all Juggalos?" Cadence asked excitedly.

"Nah, nah. We're not Juggalos," said the larger and more talkative of the two. The bigger, less attractive one did most of the talking and appeared to be the brains of the operation.

"Really? 'Cause we were at the Gathering last year and we saw all kinds of tattoos like those," Cadence relayed.

With those magic words, the young man's charade dissipated and they threw themselves into discussing every Juggalo's favorite topic: Juggalos. (To be fair, that had become arguably my favorite topic at that point as well.) As he aimlessly fondled an outsize bag of weed, the older Juggalo relayed the story behind the Hatchetman with the cane. He'd gotten it in honor of a buddy of his whose foot had become so horrifically mangled in an accident that it twisted backwards and died not long afterward.

The Hatchetman-with-the-cane tattoo couldn't help but remind me of the Hatchetman tattoo the Juggalo with the thousand-yard stare sported at the Greyhound bus station in Ohio. I began to wonder how many Hatchetman tattoos commemorated dead friends. As I wandered over to the bathroom, my imagination was suddenly inundated with images of dead Juggalos. Suddenly all those Hatchetman tattoos I'd seen at the

Gathering and at Hallowicked began to take on a ghostly, ele-giac quality.

Juggalos die disproportionately young. They die because they are overwhelmingly poor and lack access to good health care and live in impoverished neighborhoods in broken homes riddled with domestic violence and child abuse. They die because they drink and drive and take the kind of foolish, reckless chances young people habitually take because they can't see past the next ten minutes, let alone the next ten years.

The Dark Carnival's moral component takes on a new urgency in this context. For an eighteen-year-old Juggalo, death isn't something that will happen eventually, to you and your parents and the people you love somewhere down the road. It's not an abstract specter. It's something that lurks around every corner.

Insane Clown Posse sparked one of its habitual tidal waves of bad publicity when it threatened legal action against the Upright Citizens Brigade Theatre in Los Angeles, which advertised a "Funeral for a Motherfucking Dead Juggalo Baby," ostensibly hosted by Violent J and Shaggy 2 Dope.

The show riffed on a very ugly and public confrontation between a Juggalo whose baby had died and the nefarious forces of Juggalo Holocaust, and while I find the idea of threatening legal action against a satirical troupe abhorrent, I'm equally disturbed by the glib sadism of trying to glean cheap laughs out of something as sad as the death of an infant.

When I got back from the bathroom, the stouter Juggalo passed me a joint and showed me footage he'd shot on his Black-Berry of the storage facility where he lived. He'd pimped it out as nicely as anyone can trick out a space designed to temporarily house inanimate objects.

"Dude, you've got mushrooms *all* over your face," he said to his buddy.

The happy-go-lucky friend simply smiled a big shit-eating grin and said, "Dude, I found a whole eighth of mushrooms just sitting there, waiting for me in the fucking Porta-Potty. That, dude," he said before pausing dramatically, "is why *I* am a karma *billionaire*." Karma billionaire: What a lovely concept.

Throughout my trip there were times when I felt fucked by fate and times when I felt like a karma billionaire: I felt like a karma billionaire when I discovered that one of Phish's managers was Jason Colton, the brother of writer and editor Michael Colton, a man I'd worked with a decade earlier on a website called Modern Humorist.

It was a fairly shaky in, but when Jason texted to ask if I wanted to meet up with him for a beer the next day, I figured I had nothing to lose.

The manager knew of my unsuccessful appeals to Phish's publicist for press tickets, and while he never said so explicitly, he seemed understandably skeptical of my motives. Shit, I would have been skeptical of my motives. They were impure, perhaps terminally so, but not where Phish was concerned.

Having trawled along the gutter of the Phish experience for weeks on Greyhound buses and in sad little motel rooms, it felt exhilarating to suddenly have insider access. Jason had a stash of VIP wristbands to the Sierra Nevada beer tent at his disposal and invited us to help ourselves. Having read about the decadence and debauchery of Phish during the hedonistic years, I was both disappointed and relieved to find the VIP tent a fairly sedate affair. The sticky-sweet smell of corporate synergy lay heavy in the air as Phish toasted a fortuitous and symbiotic business relationship with Sierra Nevada, consummated with its signature Foam beer ("Foam" is both the name of a Phish song and, unfortunately for the folks at Sierra Nevada, a generally undesirable characteristic in a beer), and Cadence, Jason, and I kibitzed with a master brewer who was just a little too handsome and stared at Cadence just a little too intently.

Then a titanic force swept into the tent looking like an exact cross between Jerry Garcia and Dr. Demento, with a little Santa Claus thrown in for good measure. Jason greeted him warmly. The gentleman immediately apologized to all assembled if he didn't recognize us the next time we ran into each other, as he was suffering from Face Blindness.

I'd never heard of Face Blindness, a medical condition that makes it impossible for sufferers to recognize faces even upon encountering them countless times. Within the context of Phish World, that had to be a particularly vexing condition. Where else are you regularly called upon to remember the faces of people you've known for an hour and a half from within a sea of similarly shaggy, ecstatically smiling faces? Community is everything in Phish World, so being unable to even recognize people had to be a terrible, terrible handicap in every sense.

This eccentric gentleman hadn't let his unfortunate condition keep him from making a substantive contribution to Phish World. For close to two decades, he's held an unofficial position as the group's resident timekeeper. Since the early 1990s, he's timed out every song of every concert from his vantage point in the front row of every Phish show. Actually, that's not entirely true: For a good five-year period he was banned from the front row of Phish shows because Anastasio found him and his time-keeping distracting.

For a group and scene synonymous with hedonism, Phish is incredibly conducive to obsessive-compulsive geekiness. The Internet played a huge role in spreading the band's popularity. Long before other groups figured the Internet out, Phish was smartly playing both sides of the equation; they were huge live draws, but they were just as massive in the shadowy world of file sharing. Phish dominated and continue to dominate two fields that allowed them to remain invisible to the vast majority of rock 'n' roll fans. They never sold massive units or got much in the way of radio play, so they became secret superstars, giants in their field and nonentities to much of the world.

When Jason asked if Cadence and I would be interested in going backstage to check out Phish's radio station, The Bunny, my eyes grew as big as saucers and I beamed, "Oh, God, yes."

Backstage was a lot like the VIP tent: incongruously good, wholesome fun. It was decked out like a proper campground with lots of nice trailers for the band members and their families. The radio station occupied a funky little trailer with wood panel-ing and some very agreeable radio jocks inside.

Then came words of magic. "Hey," Jason began casually, "they're about to give out the trophy to the woman who won the race. Would you like to watch from the side of the stage?" I was, at this point, more or less sober, but the moment that magical query was asked, I instantly felt high as a kite.

If I had been asked if I wanted to go backstage at a Phish show three years earlier, it would have been an empty gesture.

But now it was absolutely exhilarating being at the nexus of that much positive energy. It felt a little like being inside a nuclear bomb or the eye of a hurricane. I stood there alongside Cadence as we looked out at tens of thousands of happy revelers and sideways at four ravishingly unassuming middle-aged men who somehow seemed simultaneously wonderfully human and godlike. That is the essence of Phish's divinity: On a really good night they play like gods but walk the earth as mere mortals. They don't just look like mere mortals: With the exception of Trey, who looks like a Muppet version of Jesus, every last one of them looks like your high school vice principal.

After the prize was given, Jason asked if we'd like to go to the other side of the stage to catch a few more songs. I was torn between not wanting to outstay my welcome and not wanting to waste the opportunity of a lifetime. I only wished my friend Billy from the road could have been there to share it with me. After all the valleys we'd experienced together pinballing across the great spooky Midwest and East Coast, it would have been wonderful to have been able to share a peak with him as well.

We stood at the side of the stage, utterly transfixed, while Phish began their second set of the day with the thematically appropriate "Runaway Jim" before Trey announced the winners of the Runaway Jim 5K race, then segueing into "McGrupp and the Watchful Hosemasters," "Axilla I," and "Birds of a Feather."

They weren't my favorite Phish songs, not by a long shot, but I nevertheless felt unbelievably blessed to experience them from such a privileged vantage point. In a strange sort of way it felt as if everything I had been experiencing was mere preamble leading up to that particular moment.

To paraphrase the title of a Phish song Anastasio turned into an appropriately epic symphonic album, at a truly transcendent show time turns elastic and fans are temporarily liberated from the tyranny of the clock.

We stop being prisoners of time, and for a brief, drugged-up idyll become its master. We are put in touch with the timeless, the unknowable, the divine: pure consciousness. Throughout my travels I experienced moments like that, moments that I never wanted to end. The nice thing about being at a Phish festival is that at the beginning of the day, the concept of a show that will never end seems like an endlessly appealing and strangely palatable option. On that Saturday, for example, Phish began by playing a nearly two-hour-long opening set that would be a more than respectable night's performance for most bands. For Phish during Super Ball, however, that meant they were barely warming up. By the time they finished playing a wholly improvised secret fourth set with Page on the theremin deep into the wee small hours of the morning, Phish had played for just under six hours, rendering it one of the longest performances in its history—yet it still wasn't enough.

That evening I met a gentleman named Andy Bernstein, who had edited and helped compile *The Pharmer's Almanac: The Unofficial Guide to Phish,* a seminal reference book on Phish, before becoming executive director of HeadCount, an organization he cofounded with Marc Brownstein, bassist for the Disco Biscuits, that had registered hundreds of thousands of young voters at shows.

Bernstein had a sweet-ass trailer that was visited that night by Steve Pollak, a songwriter better known to Phish fans under his moniker Dude of Life. Along with his friend Trey, Pollak had written some of Phish's best and most beloved and memorable songs, including "Fluffhead" and "Suzy Greenberg." Despite the auspicious place Pollak occupied in Phish mythology—in the early 1990s he'd even recorded a solo album with Phish as his backing band—he had an air of humility that impressed me disproportionately.

Consciously or unconsciously, I think we all expect impressive people to be unbearably arrogant and self-absorbed and are surprised and delighted when they prove otherwise. Pollak worked as a special education teacher, and I would imagine he's far too modest to ever tell his students, "Do you realize how fucking excited you guys would be to be in my presence if you were Phish fans? Seriously, among a certain subsection of the general public I am, at the very least, a minor deity." Shit, I felt honored to be in his laconic presence and Bernstein's as well.

A feeling of absolute peace and transcendence swept over me when Phish closed out a remarkable festival with "The Star-Spangled Banner" as July 3 turned into July 4 and fireworks exploded high above Watkins Glen. After a summer of weird vibes and anxious times, everything was seeming to come together perfectly. For the time being.

THE GATHERING OF THE
JUGGALOS 2011:
BANG! POW! BOOM!

Super Ball IX proved a masterpiece of planning and execution. Everything had gone right. The same could not quite be said of the next festival on my schedule: the almighty Gathering of the Juggalos. I had a date with destiny in just over a month. I hoped I was finally ready. I went to my first Gathering of the

Juggalos as a curious outsider. By the time I returned to the sacred ground of Cave-in-Rock, I was ready to announce to the world that I was down with the clown till I'm dead in the ground.

I am not too proud to concede that there was some small, greasepainted corner of my soul that greeted the prospect of a return to the Gathering of the Juggalos with feverish anticipation. For something strange and unexpected happened between my first and second Gatherings: At the risk of losing what little journalistic credibility I have left, I came to enjoy listening to the music of Insane Clown Posse. Make of that what you will. You might be tempted to write my newfound appreciation off as a critical case of Stockholm Syndrome. Alternately, you can attribute my affection to the untreated head injury I incurred at Bethel Woods. In that case, feel free to dismiss the following as the incoherent rambling of the pop-culture world's answer to *Regarding Henry.*

Violent J pointedly did not advise listening to his group's music. This speaks to a strange duality regarding the role music plays in the Juggalo subculture: It's at once its epicenter and strangely irrelevant. Without the music of ICP, the Gathering and Juggalos would not exist, but Juggalo subculture has transcended music to the point where you can lose yourself in the iconography and ideas and lifestyle without paying too much attention to the music itself.

I'm not going to posit Insane Clown Posse as great, misunderstood artists even as I feel they have been greatly misunderstood over the course of their decades in the spotlight. Praise the Clowns as dumb fun, and you shortchange the genuine ambition and vision of the Joker's Cards and the Dark Carnival. Highlight the ambition and vision of the Dark Carnival, and you end up overselling a guilty pleasure. Praise the group as a Barnumesque racket, and you risk rendering the music irrelevant. Being down with the clown can be a tricky business.

Listening to the duo's 1992 debut *Carnival of Carnage,* it's easy to see why the group was received as warmly as a NAMBLA delegation at a Boy Scout convention by critics, MTV, hip-hop radio, and other gatekeepers of culture. There's a rawness to the album that's at once jarring and strangely seductive, a primitiveness that marks it as outsider art.

In an endearingly amateurish attempt at an ominous voice, the narrator of the album's intro track speaks of a gentle night in "your town," where the peace and tranquility are about to be destroyed by the titular circus of depravity and devastation. He speaks of an evil creeping in from the distance, slithering through quiet streets, and confronting a terrified populace doomed to pay the ultimate price for a trip to the carnival.

"Intro" establishes some enduring themes within the ICP canon: the contrast between illusion and reality and the need to comfort the afflicted and afflict the comfortable. In *Carnival of Carnage,* the urban poor bring the horrors of the ghetto to the ritziest suburbs. They're the demonic unleashed id of the suffering underclass turned monstrous and eviscerating, a sentient plague upon those who exploit and control the downtrodden. *Carnival of Carnage* similarly establishes a pronounced anti-redneck bias in ICP's music that finds its purest expression in "Your Rebel Flag" (as in "fuck your"). Here, as elsewhere, Violent J's cartoon aggression is undercut by ingratiating naïveté; according to *Behind the Paint,* Violent J was moved to write songs like "Rebel Flag" and "Redneck Hoe" because he was so horrified by the racism he'd encountered while visiting his brother down South. J writes that before visiting his brother he had never experienced racism before, either firsthand or indirectly, and consequently was shocked and horrified by it.

By the time of 1997's *The Great Milenko* Insane Clown Posse had shaken off the amateurish sociopathology of *Carnival of Carnage* and found its growling, rasping, ridiculous, and darkly comic voice. "Hokus Pokus" marries an elastic bass groove reminiscent of Cypress Hill's "How I Could Just Kill a Man" with carnival organ and demented lyrics about walking into a Gypsy's tent with a food stamp and walking out with a magical lamp. It's a great hip-hop song, but more than anything it's a great pop song, with an infectious sing-along chorus that takes up valuable real estate in the mind, then claims squatter's rights and refuses to leave. Folks laughing derisively at ICP don't seem to realize that Insane Clown Posse spends much of its time laughing at itself, its fans, and the gothic universe it has created. With the possible exception of the "Miracles" video, Insane Clown Posse is supposed to be funny. That's the ICP that resonates and speaks to me, the macabre dark humorists transforming everything into a sinister, self-deprecating joke.

On "What Is a Juggalo?" for example, Violent J and Shaggy 2 Dope paint an affectionate, gently mocking portrait of their fan base as sloppy drunks, perverts, and out-and-out lunatics. ICP take nothing seriously on the song, including each other's verses.

At one point Violent J raps that a Juggalo'll "eat Monopoly and shit out Connect 4," a line that flummoxes Shaggy 2 Dope to the point that he actually interrupts his own rap to complain that Violent J's lyric doesn't make any sense. In "What Is a Juggalo?" Insane Clown Posse has good-natured fun with just about every element of their fan base, including their education. When the duo insists, "What is a Juggalo? He's a graduate," their claim is met by the lonely, mocking sounds of crickets chirping before the duo is forced to concede, "At least he got a job/He's not a dumb putz/He works for himself scratching his nuts." Everyone has fun at the expense of Juggalos, even Insane Clown Posse. *Especially* Insane Clown Posse.

The monster hook and catchy production of "Down with the Clown" betray one of Insane Clown Posse's guiltiest secrets: The most reviled horrorcore band in existence is actually a nifty pop outfit. The Insane Clown Posse-versus-the-mainstream dichotomy has more to do with ideology and marketing than it does with the music itself, which can be pretty goddamn infectious if you open your mind to it.

I came to unironically enjoy Insane Clown Posse's music because it's funny and catchy and gloriously unpretentious, but I also responded to its romanticization of a weirdly specific form of poverty. Even if the humor and class consciousness of Insane Clown Posse leave you cold, it's hard not to admire the conceptual ambition of launching an ongoing, seemingly open-ended narrative that plays out over the course of an entire decade.

The mythology of the Dark Carnival culminates in "Thy Unveiling," the final track off *The Wraith: Shangri-La* and the most important track in Insane Clown Posse's discography and the Dark Carnival mythology. Everything leads up to "Thy Unveiling." Everything.

On "Thy Unveiling," the past takes on a physical presence as Violent J references the five Joker's Cards leading up to that pivotal moment before dramatically announcing that time is up. The time for obfuscation is passed. The moment has arrived when all will be revealed. Pulling back the curtain further, Insane Clown Posse reveal that they'd been dropping hints and messages throughout their albums that most of their fans never picked up on because they "stuck 'em in subliminally with the wicked shit around them."

The song mounts in volume and intensity as Insane Clown Posse dramatically announce that the Carnival is more than the sum of its parts. It's bigger than Psychopathic Records. It's bigger than Insane Clown Posse. It's an idea as big as the universe itself, if not bigger, since it extends deep into the afterlife and other worlds. The song builds and builds and builds until J unleashes the central revelation behind Insane Clown Posse's music: "When we speak of Shangri-La, what you think we mean? Truth is we follow GOD!!! We've always been behind him/The carnival is GOD and may all Juggalos find him."

In *Behind the Paint,* J writes that the revelation of the final Joker's Card was so powerful it reduced fans to tears, but I suspect a goodly percentage of the group's fans felt ripped off. *This* was the big statement the group was making? *This* was their big manifesto? Follow God? Wasn't that what every fucking authority figure they'd ever encountered told them? And now *that* was the ultimate message of ICP? Follow God?

Insane Clown Posse inherently acknowledges the inevitable disappointment of Juggalos when it chants, "We're not sorry that we tricked you!" on "Thy Unveiling" itself. "Thy Unveiling" is a gospel anthem unlike any other, and not just because it's littered with profanity and references to previous Insane Clown Posse songs. It's the Gospel of the Scrub, the Holy Book of Juggalo. Insane Clown Posse brings the full weight of the Dark Carnival mythology to bear on "Thy Unveiling," crafting a weirdly if characteristically profane rap-operatic mission statement that thunders with pop-messianic purpose.

By the time 2009's *Bang! Pow! Boom!* arrived, Insane Clown Posse was ready to embrace its inner pop star. The title track is a groovy throwback number that finds ecstasy in a bleak moral reckoning. It's Insane Clown Posse in microcosm: finding the joy in the macabre and the celebration in the gothic. Also, it's catchy as fuck.

This brings us to "Miracles." That song changed my life. Without "Miracles," there would be no Gathering of the Juggalos for me, no Hallowickeds, no Joker's Cards. I would have missed the whole surreal circus. I don't know whether to be grateful or rue the day I ever heard that song.

When I first listened to "Miracles," all I heard was the mind-boggling incongruity of violent clowns calling attention to the wonder and mystery of our world with hilarious earnestness. I grooved to the surreal juxtaposition of profane language expressing clumsily sacred sentiments. "Miracles" awkwardly but gloriously captures Insane Clown Posse's childlike sense of wonder, its profound if cockeyed appreciation for the endless bounty we've been given. "Miracles" may have made Insane Clown Posse even more of a laughingstock than before, but is there really anything wrong with finding the fantastic and transcendent in the every-day, in imploring your fans to look at a corrupt material world and see the timeless and the divine? True, the message of "Mira-cles" would probably be more powerful and better received if it didn't also contain bizarre non sequiturs about pelicans trying to eat cell phones or angry demands to know how fucking magnets work, but on "Miracles" the duo's intentions are nothing if not admirable. Shaggy 2 Dope's line about not wanting to talk to a scientist was ridiculed as an ignorant antiscience screed, but— and I will concede that this is a little generous—I think the line is critical of those who look at the wonders of the world and see *only* science, without leaving any room for awe or the divine.

But more than anything, what I responded to in Insane Clown Posse's music was the exhilarating sense of freedom I experienced at the Gathering: freedom from shame, freedom from self-consciousness, freedom from even the foggiest notion of good taste. A world of freedom opens up when you decide to stop caring about what the world thinks of you. Musically and otherwise, Insane Clown Posse take full advantage of the free-dom that comes with having nothing left to lose, with having been mocked or derided from the very beginning.

For the twelfth Annual Gathering of the Juggalos, Insane Clown Posse headlined a 1990s hip-hop head's wet dream. It's as if Insane Clown Posse shuffled a pack of *Yo! MTV Raps* cards from 1992 and picked out the festival's entertainment at ran-dom. So minor West Coast legend DJ Quik (can you be a minor legend? If so, then Quik is definitely it) is joined on the bill by slang-spitting Bay Area linguist E-40, former stockbroker/Black Nationalist rapper Paris (best known for his controversial single "Bush Killa"), West Coast gangsta rap pioneer turned children's entertainment mogul Ice Cube, crunk kingpin and hoarse-shouting enthusiast Lil Jon, once-controversial early 1990s pop-rap megastars Vanilla Ice and MC Hammer, R&B superstar turned professional fuck-up Bobby Brown, and far too many other big names and fascinating stories to go into. Tila Tequila had threatened to shut down the Gathering but it had returned bigger, fiercer, weirder, and more defiant than ever.

Between my first and second Gatherings, I had forgotten how impossible the roads leading to Cave-in-Rock are to navigate. Hog Rock, the campground where the festival is held, is so remote it doesn't even have an address. Streetlights are nonexistent. The road is unpaved and uneven. We drove past a busted-down old shed with graffiti crudely reading WHOOP WHOOP and JUGGALO and knew we were officially in Juggalo country once we saw a steady stream of cops pulling folks over and putting them away in hand-cuffs. The police were out in full force that year, though there were massive limits to their powers. They could pull over and arrest anyone they wanted, but since the local jail housed only eight or nine people (this is Cave-In-Rock, Illinois, we're talking about, after all), pretty much everyone had to be released at some point.

Behind us in line to receive our press passes, a naked woman stood looking bored with studied nonchalance, affording the Gathering a full-on glimpse of the gaudy burst of vaginal jewelry decorating her pierced clitoris and the Hitler mustache line of her pubic hair. I should point out that Cadence made that observation, not I. It's remarkable how quickly you become jaded at the sight of naked flesh of all varieties at the Gathering. And, oh, sweet Lord, do you see naked flesh of all varieties. It's an empowering realm where women who weigh three hundred pounds can strut around topless and win only approving grins and cries of, "Whoop! Whoop!" from their compatriots.

Public nudity is a not insignificant part of what makes the Gathering the Gathering. The transgressive allure of the festival is that it's a world without consequences, where everything is allowed and the only real imperative is to not harm thy fellow Juggalo or lose thy shit.

Of course plenty of folks blatantly ignore the imperative not to harm thy fellow Juggalo. Just about every year at the Gathering somebody gets stabbed or killed or winds up dead. There's a strange air of inevitability to it. If you bring together thousands of largely poor, uneducated people without opportunities or resources and get them drunk and high on just about everything, then some violence is going to occur. It's just going to happen no matter the safeguards put in place, and, to be fair, there are very few safeguards put in place.

I think it would behoove Violent J to just kind of throw that out at his yearly seminar, to say, "Look, guys. We're all going to have a blast here at the Gathering. We're going to make memories to last a lifetime, and also someone is going to get stabbed, probably over a drug deal. So while enjoying yourself at the festival, take care not to get stabbed."

The Gathering isn't just about the yearly stabbing. It's also about performing, and many of the performers aren't onstage. They're people who've chosen to make a spectacle of themselves for this very special occasion and have pieced together papier-mâché hatchets and homemade Dark Lotus costumes and more jailhouse tattoos than can be found in most major correctional facilities. At the Gathering of the Juggalos, you do the wrong thing just because you can. Hell, you do the wrong thing because that's pretty much what's expected of you.

Perhaps that explains why a perfectly nondescript U-Haul van left the parking lot of the Gathering with a naked woman hanging out of both windows. It's the kind of thing you don't see every day, except at the Gathering of the Juggalos it's *exactly* the kind of thing you see every day. At the Gathering, everything is reversed. The question becomes less "Why would I show strangers my naked body?" than "What am I doing wearing clothes? Who am I, the fucking queen of England? I might as well have that Great Milenko neck tattoo laser-removed if I'm going to get that highfalutin and fancified."

On her way to park her car, Cadence received several requests to show her tits.

"This early in the festival, boys?"

"We'll hit you up later," they replied.

"First time at the Gathering?" asked a woman behind us when she noticed a look of mild surprise on Cadence's face as she gawked at the girl with the Hitler-mustache pubic hair, clad only in furry boots and smoking a cigarette.

"No, but I just didn't expect to know so much about that stranger's vaginal piercings," Cadence replied.

The media presence seemed way up this year. The press could be profiled from a hundred feet away by their stylish haircuts, fedoras, and cynical air of ironic detachment. The Gathering of the Juggalos was no longer the secret it once had been. Via Twitter I hooked up with an affable young man named Christopher Weingarten, who was covering the Gathering for MTV.com. Once upon a time MTV was Insane Clown Posse's bête noire. They were the gatekeepers who stubbornly refused to let Insane Clown Posse penetrate the ranks of pop stardom. MTV used to transform unknowns into stars. During Insane Clown Posse's late-1990s commercial heyday, MTV took established stars with a huge, dedicated fan base, millions in album sales, and an entire subculture marching in lockstep behind them and treated them like unknowns.

This was a new day, however. Weingarten approached the Gathering of the Juggalos and Insane Clown Posse with the same attitude he seemed to bring to everything: an open mind, guileless enthusiasm, and infectious curiosity. He didn't drink or use drugs, but that didn't keep him exuding childlike enthusiasm over just about everything, from getting to see some of his favorite overlooked 1990s rap legends in an unfamiliar context to the Faygo snow cones and carnival goodies like popcorn and cotton candy. He was quite literally an overgrown kid at a carnival.

Weingarten's open mind reflected a gradual softening in the media's attitude toward Insane Clown Posse. It's an old truism that everyone grows respectable with age except whores and politicians, and while it would still be a stretch to call Insane Clown Posse respectable, the longevity of these ridiculous men and their carny arsenal of low-rent gimmicks has earned them grudging respect from a media and culture that have historically held them in contempt.

Part of this is attributable to a mellowing in the group itself. In *Behind the Paint,* a swaggering and inveterately anti-authoritarian Violent J memorably writes that he "gives no fuck" if his theoretical offspring slapped the shit out of a teacher. These days doting dad and happy husband J tweets ecstatically about his son's victory in the Cub Scouts' Pinewood Derby and makes homemade music videos starring his adorable son (dubbed Violent JJ, of course) and daughter Ruby. *Saturday Night Live* ran so many parodies of Insane Clown Posse, "Miracles," and the Gathering of the Juggalos that the eminently respectable folks at the *New York Times* ran an oral history ("Fools' Gold: An Oral History of the Insane Clown Posse Parodies") on April 26, 2010. True, it was as a joke and as fodder for satire, but they had penetrated the realm of mainstream media.

In an even more auspicious development, Jack White of the White Stripes lent his stamp of approval to the duo when he produced a single for Insane Clown Posse ("Leck Mich Im Arsch/ Mountain Girl") through his Third Man Records imprint. An icon of underground cool who had also produced Loretta Lynn's breathtaking and universally revered comeback album *Van Lear Rose* decided that the band was worth his time and energy.

Insane Clown Posse haven't just survived. They've thrived. The record industry has crumbled, major labels teeter on the brink of extinction, yet Insane Clown Posse's culture and business and mythology have stood the test of time and birthed multiple generations of Juggalos. That alone is enough to engender long-overdue props even from folks who consider the group a crime against music and an affront to all that is good and decent in the world.

Upon entering the festival, Cadence and I rambled over to a food truck where a Juggalo in a wifebeater and jeans woozily zigzagged up to us.

"Are you guys, you know?" he then thrust a finger through his closed hand in a crude pantomime of sexual intercourse.

We replied sheepishly that we were, indeed, doing what his crude hand gesture was supposed to represent and he mumbled back, "That's all right. I mean, she's got boobs and stuff and that's good."

The man was the subject of one of the most popular games of the Festival: How is that person still standing? Alternately: How is that person still conscious? Everywhere you looked, people staggered and bumped into each other yet somehow remained inexplicably upright. At a watering hole called Spazzmotic Bar, where people drank booze they'd smuggled into the festival (sales of alcohol were officially forbidden) and cut up lines of cocaine on park tables, Cadence and I watched with rapt fascination as a heroically sweaty fat man clad only in a pair of loose-fitting sweatpants stumbled in weird little sumo steps. There was a strange nobility to the man's inexplicably successful quest to remain vertical.

At a lunch table, we talked to a pair of Juggalos from Colorado. They had been driving up to the festival and gotten pulled over by the cops. They were busted with an ounce and a half of pot, handcuffed, and put in the back of a police car before being let go on the condition they returned the next month to pay a ticket.

The boyfriend toiled as an assistant manager at a Sonic's. His girlfriend had dropped out of school and lived with her parents but nursed vague goals to go back to school and get certification in teaching sign language. She described her aspirations with the slightly embarrassed self-consciousness poor people sometimes feel when describing goals and aspirations they fear might forever be out of their grasp.

The Gathering has a way of evening everything out. Once upon a time MC Hammer and Vanilla Ice battled for supremacy over the pop charts. Hammer was once big enough to mount a very public challenge to Michael Jackson's throne as the King of Pop. (Jackson, meanwhile, had the good sense and solid judgment to ignore him.) Hammer embodied hip-hop-pop sellouts to such an extent that when Violent J imagined himself and Shaggy 2 Dope selling out on "Down with the Clown," he envisioned himself "sportin' some Hammer pants/kick-steppin' with Shaggs and tryna dance!"

At the Gathering of the Juggalos, where failure was celebrated as much, if not more, than success, it could be hard to tell the two apart. In their own strange way, both Vanilla Ice and MC Hammer triumphed. Longtime friend of the family Vanilla Ice used his appearance to announce he'd officially signed to Psychopathic Records, while Hammer's performance proved an unlikely highlight of the entire festival.

Hammer's once booming entourage had been reduced to a skeleton crew. Back in the day, Hammer drove himself to bankruptcy putting on ridiculous extravaganzas that rivaled anything the rock world came up with. Now he was cursed by the gods to try to put on a Vegas spectacle on a Reno budget.

At the Gathering, Hammer performed an energetic set that found him wandering into the crowd extensively and working up a James Brown–level sweat, but his set didn't really come alive until he exited and Juggalos began climbing onstage with expressions of delight mixed with confusion and uncertainty. They'd made the leap onto the stage, but they had no idea what to do with their newfound power. So they fell upon an old standby. "Family! Family!" they started chanting. It was a moment of joyful anarchy and a deliciously literal representation of what the Psychopathic/Juggalo ethos is all about: The fans are as important as the acts. When Juggalos chant "Family," they're celebrating themselves and their connection to one another as much as, if not more than, their alliance to two greasepaint enthusiasts from Michigan.

Then something glorious happened. The telltale first few bars of "U Can't Touch This" came on and the Juggalos onstage and in the crowd went nuts. A song that once epitomized the slick emptiness of mainstream commercial hip-hop at its most facile and mercenary had been transformed into an unlikely anthem for fans of the most hated band in the world. "U Can't Touch This" now belonged to everyone. It had been transformed into a motherfucking Juggalo anthem, of all things, and a motley aggregation of face-painted lunatics was having the time of their goddamn lives. I am not too proud to concede that there's a big part of me that wishes I'd been onstage dancing alongside Hammer when he performed it.

Busta Rhymes is one of the most combustible live performers in all of popular music, but his set couldn't help but feel like a letdown following "U Can't Touch This." In a bid to compensate, Rhymes laid it on thick with the crowd, describing the performance he'd just given as a defining moment in his career and the crowd as unlike any he'd ever played for. In a bit of false humility, Rhymes all but begged to be invited back next year as if he were some unknown angling for a big break and not a megastar picking up a giant paycheck.

On Friday night our trip to see Lil Jon expectorate hoarse shouts was interrupted by a pair of second-stage performers who spotted our press badges and seized upon us a fortuitous forum to air their grievances.

The man was in his early forties and had a billy goat scruff and eyes alive with righteous indignation. He performed as the Real V3NOM alongside his wife, MissCyainide, a heavyset twenty-one-year-old with tattoo tears on her face. They had come early to the Gathering to help set things up, as they do every year. This year marked their debut as performers, but the excitement of being able to actually play at the big show was tempered by the disappointment he felt when he and his wife were denied an artist's pass and had to pay their own way.

The Real V3NOM was an old-school Juggalo from way back. To MissCyainide, the Real V3NOM served as a one-man crash course in all things Juggalo. They had met when they were both at a county fair in full Juggalo makeup. MissCyainide said to one of her girlfriends, "Who is that hot Juggalo over there?" The rest was history.

There was something oppressively adorable about the couple. They had matching Hatchetman and Hatchetwoman tattoos on their forearms so that when they're combined it looks like they're hugging instead of, you know, killing each other with hatchets.

Being denied an artist's pass was a major blow to the man's ego. He'd put in his work in the Juggalo trenches, helping out wherever he could, and now he was being treated like a mere fan. It was disrespectful, but he still couldn't shake his love for the music and the culture. The man still flew the flag proudly, but there was clearly some part of him that wondered if all this time and energy and emotional investment were for naught.

Deadly Poisons, as the couple were collectively known when they performed together, still loved ICP. They still loved the Gathering. They still loved Juggalos. But they were disappointed by the state of the scene and the band that fuels it. The Real V3NOM, the true believer, saw fewer and fewer of his kind out there. He sneered dismissively at what he called "Merchalos," newcomers who dug the gear but couldn't care less about the band, its music, and its message. As with seemingly all subcultures, the old guard was innately suspicious of newcomers.

"What kind of music do you play?" I inquired.

"I guess I would call what we perform like 'conscious rap,' like rap that means something and talks about real stuff that we're all going through like," MissCyanide said, and then began rapping while I stood there awkwardly.

The Drug Bridge horrified the couple. The Real V3NOM smoked weed because it helped him with his back pain, but he was understandably disturbed by the sight of shirtless seventeen-year-old kids holding cardboard signs advertising coke, weed, Oxy, and pills. It was a gauntlet of sketchy characters peddling illicit wares, to me kind of glorious in its own seedy fashion, in its inimitably ugly-beautiful Juggalo kind of way. But it pissed the Real V3NOM off. "Why the fuck are there people on the bridge trying to sell crack to a Juggalo?" he asked angrily. "Why are there fucking families on there selling drugs together?"

The Real V3NOM felt that ICP was slowing down and preparing to retire so that they could launch the next generation of Psychopathic Artists. He found that troubling. Insane Clown Posse was the linchpin that held everything together.

In a sentiment that was echoed throughout the Gathering, the Real V3NOM felt the Gathering had gotten too mainstream, that it was chasing pop fans who never in a million years would travel to the *Deliverance* country of Cave-in-Rock, Illinois, for an opportunity to see Ice Cube. No, they came to see the wicked shit.

The couple lived in what they described as a horrible little shit town in big, weird-ass Ohio called Coshocton (which sounds less like a town than a disease), where they were predictably ostracized and ridiculed. It would be hard to imagine a less commercial proposition than a middle-aged white man and his zaftig wife recording conscious hip-hop for Insane Clown Posse fans from the hip-hop mecca of Coshocton, Ohio. Yet this pair was soldiering on all the same, united in their belief in themselves, their abilities, and each other. They took the Dark Carnival as seriously as anything involving Moon Bounces, helicopter rides, and constant cries of "Show me your titties!" can be taken. That's why the rejection stung so badly.

The Real V3NOM groused that Violent J drove a 2006 Escalade while he drove a busted-ass hooptie from the 1980s. There were savage iniquities all around. Yet Deadly Poisons flew the flag all the same.

Next to Deadly Poisons stood a quiet young man who looked a lot like Jesus with his long light-brown hair, beard, and general air of mellowness. He looked like Jesus but he also looked like someone who had gotten lost on his way to a Dave Matthews Band show and ended up in Cave-in-Rock, Illinois.

The young man came to the music of ICP in a backwards way. As a kid in southern Michigan, he was into wrestling and knew Violent J and Shaggy 2 Dope solely as wrestlers in the WWE. Then one day he discovered *The Great Milenko* and was shocked to discover those weird wrestlers with the face paint also had a sideline in hip-hop. He bought his first album and fell in love.

The man had been dubbed "Sexy Jesus" for good reason: He loved Insane Clown Posse but also thought a lot of Juggalos were losers. When Cadence asked him why he didn't have any ICP tattoos, he replied, "In case I ever want to go into the corporate world or move up in my job at all, it would really harm me if I had too many visible tattoos or piercings."

That kind of common sense and reasonable thinking had no place in the Gathering. Nor did Sexy Jesus's measured appraisal of a scene he enjoys but finds fundamentally depressing. I immediately pegged him as a pothead, but he told us that he never smoked weed. He never even drank. He just liked the music and the company and hanging out with his friends from Texas he gets to see once a year. And Faygo. He really, really dug Faygo.

The man defied every stereotype and preconception about Juggalos. He was handsome and unadorned. He didn't drink or smoke pot and he thought seriously about his future. He was in complete control of his faculties and just wanted to hang out and have a good time.

Cadence and I agreed that if Sexy Jesus had been born in Alaska and was rich instead of poor, he'd be a hippie rather than a Juggalo. He was particularly annoyed that ICP put out three different collector's editions of *Bang! Pow! Boom!* There was one with a blue cover. Then there was one with a green cover, and finally a red cover. Each had a different intro and a different bonus track, but they were otherwise the same.

As Sexy Jesus noted wryly, "If you know one thing about Juggalos, it's that they're broke. As far as I know, rich Juggalos don't exist, so it's asking an awful lot of fans to buy three nearly identical albums, especially in a record-industry climate where *nobody* but *nobody* is buying albums anymore, especially not CDs."

ICP is rich, and their fans are often very poor. This allows Juggalos to live vicariously through the larger-than-life exploits of their heroes, but on some level jealousy has to sink in, especially considering how many Juggalos would literally murder someone with a hatchet to join their ranks.

J acknowledged the limitations to what ICP could do for their fans when I spoke to him. "Everybody always talks about how they wish we could all live together all the time, and I always say if we were mad rich we'd buy like an old hotel somewhere downtown, with like ten floors and thirty rooms on each floor, and we'd just fucking rent them out for cheap and have them be a Juggalo haven. Where all the Juggalos are living in every room, we'd just hang out and go room to room, it'd just be awesome. But we'd have to lock the doors. We talk about that, like how dope that would be to do that one day, but I don't know if that's even legally possible, but that'd just be the shit."

Alas, those were just words, and at the end of the day Violent J would return to his lush life in Michigan and Deadly Poisons would return to Coshocton, Ohio, and immediately begin day-dreaming about the next Gathering.

Though he performed before Anybody Killa, the big star Friday night was gangsta rap pioneer Ice Cube, whose performance of "It Was a Good Day" had special resonance for the Juggalos in attendance. One of the most furtively sad feel-good songs in existence, "It Was a Good Day" is ultimately about the ephemeral nature of happiness and the way a good day for the beaten-down and oppressed is about the momentary absence of all the terrible things. "It Was a Good Day" implicitly says that happiness never lasts, but that every once in a while you can grab a few isolated moments of peace and contentment between the bullshit. What Juggalo can't relate to that?

After Cube's performance, we headed into the wrestling tent and talked to yet another man who defied stereotypes regarding Juggalos. He was a steelworker by day and a wrestler by night.

He was also an unrepentant Juggalo with the tattoos to prove it. He seemed more interested in Cadence than in me, but when she went to the bathroom he offered a surprisingly sophisticated critique of the Juggalo ethos. He began by saying that Insane Clown Posse is a metaphysical anomaly within the music industry because unlike the Grateful Dead, its central ethos isn't about worshipping the source of the music; it's bigger than that. It's not just a way of thinking, it's an ideology devoid of the specifics that, in his mind at least, get in the way of the purity of a simple idea like "Be good to others" and "Do unto others as you would have them do unto you."

"ICP is totally fake," he said. "And they're totally upfront with that. All these other rappers, they're pretending they're whatever their personas are supposed to be, but ICP, they come right out and tell you it's all an act." He'd been a Juggalo from day one and now he had a dream opportunity to wrestle for Violent J and Shaggy 2 Dope. Like Sexy Jesus, he was incongruously straight-edge in a scene ruled by drugs and alcohol.

In front of the Seminar Tent that Friday night, we struck up a conversation with a beefy, handsome young man with a wrestler's badge. He struck an oddly familiar figure, but it wasn't until we started talking to him that we realized that the nice Jewish boy from Wicker Park had wrestled at the Gathering of the Juggalos the year before as Officer Colt Cabana, the arch nemesis of Weedman and all smokers everywhere. He was there that night not to wrestle but to perform stand-up comedy along with a talented comedian buddy named Marty DeRosa. Like so many of the people I'd encountered, he defied stereotypes about fans of Insane Clown Posse: He was smart, well educated, and hosted a podcast called *Art of Wrestling*. Yet he was so down with the clown, he joked during his routine, that he'd actually gone down *on* a clown.

Cabana was opening for the evening's big headliner, Brian

Posehn. Posehn was a writer and performer on *Mr. Show* before establishing himself as the thinking man's pot comic. He's a towering aggregation of nerd obsessions—comic books, video games, heavy metal, *Mr. Show,* comedy—in sentient form.

Then this very successful pot comic did something profoundly risky. He stopped smoking pot for the sake of his daughter, his own mental health, his dignity, and his self-esteem. Then he agreed to perform at the Gathering of the Juggalos. I can only imagine they pulled the proverbial money truck into his backyard, because heaven knows there are few places less conducive to maintaining hard-won sobriety than the Gathering of the Juggalos.

Like everyone else, Posehn had heard the worst about Juggalos: They were violent. They were stupid. They threw shit. Literally. They attacked and killed people. They were a gang. So he was prepared for the worst.

Seemingly alone among the performers I saw, Posehn found a way to engage with the audience without pandering to them. "People talk a lot of shit about you guys but I've had nothing but a good time," he told the crowd with disarming sincerity. He actually seemed to mean it.

Of course, this was the Gathering. Temptation was everywhere. Eager-looking young men wearing bongs around their necks like necklaces skittered up to the stage to offer Posehn hits. He politely declined. His protests grew increasingly indignant until a young man waved a giant bag of psilocybin in Posehn's general direction and Posehn finally erupted with indignation and said something I will remember until the day I die: "Dude.

I am a grown-ass man. I'm not going to fucking do mushrooms with you."

The role of "host" at the Gathering was largely ceremonial. Hosts weren't called upon to do much more than keep the energy and volume level high, but even that seemed to be wearing on Charlie Sheen, a late addition to the Gathering of the Juggalos lineup and the event's biggest wild card. Sheen's appearance at the Gathering of the Juggalos possessed a strange element of finality. Sheen once occupied a privileged place within the center of American pop culture. He was Oliver Stone's golden boy, a beautiful man kind enough to let a goodly percentage of the American male populace live vicariously through his coke-fueled sexual misadventures. Now he'd taken his crazy act as far as it could possibly go. The homecoming king was now prostrating himself before the weird kids who sniffed glue and listened to freak music. It was a bit of an odd fit.

"Are we still whoop-whoop winning?" Sheen asked no one in particular as he anxiously gasped for words and ideas between sets.

Charlie Sheen isn't a stand-up comedian. He's not a philosopher. Onstage at Cave-in-Rock, Sheen seemed lost. He seemed like a man in need of an identity. He hit the same buzzwords hard, but they didn't have the same power or panache.

"Are we winning tonight? Are we whoop-whoop winning tonight? Can I get a whoop-whoop winning? Is the tiger blood flowing tonight? That's what I'm talking about," Sheen sputtered nervously as he stalked the stage. When cries of "Whoop! Whoop!" and "Winning!" garnered a modest response at best, Sheen shifted gears slightly and made the kind of winking drug reference your uncle might make in an attempt to seem cool. "Without any further ado, I would like to introduce the next band. I know you're looking forward to these guys because their name is also a verb. It's what all of you have been doing all day, right? *Blaze*-ing it up? Let's give a big Juggalo welcome to Blaze!"

In Cave-in-Rock, Sheen's craziness devolved into shtick. Whatever exhilarating authenticity or unpredictability he might once have possessed had alchemized into a tedious aggregation of catchphrases, buzzwords, and manufactured attitude. By the time it hit the Gathering, the ongoing freak show that was Charlie Sheen's very public career implosion and mental breakdown had overstayed its welcome. The ICP–Charlie Sheen union was as much a marriage of convenience as the ill-fated Tila Tequila–ICP alliance. Y'all know how well those tend to turn out.

THE GOOD REVEREND
BREAKS IT DOWN

Deadly Poisons eventually led us in the direction of an unusual figure within the Juggalo community named Reverend Loki, who was helping set up a makeshift performance area known as Area 17. He'd originally taken on the persona as a wrestling gimmick, but over time he'd come to embrace the role of spiritual adviser to the Juggalo nation. In the tent, the reverend discussed his first exposure to ICP.

"This is going to be a strange answer considering the type of music that the group plays," he said, "but it was a middle school dance. If you take a listen to *The Great Milenko,* the second track, after the intro, it doesn't have any cussing in it and it doesn't really talk about violence. It just talks about this mystical carnival with these spirits and whatnot showing you the truth of what's really going on with your life. That was crazy! After hearing that, I followed the CD from the DJ to whoever he borrowed it from. I asked if I could borrow it, and he never saw it again."

It was the beginning of a great love affair. "I found something that fit. I'd always loved metal and I'd always loved rock and at that time Juggalos didn't really know what it was all about. At that point, the word *Juggalo* was really just being invented at the time *Milenko* came out. The feeling the music gave you"—the reverend paused for a moment before continuing—"was magical."

It was exhilarating being part of something bigger than himself, to be an eleven-year-old who hears a song that doesn't just connect to a group or a singer but rather to a sprawling, sinister realm whose infinite mysteries were being unpacked slowly, one Joker's Card at a time.

"It's great to be part of something bigger than myself and be humble about it and enjoy it with as many people as possible around you. That, to me, is what family is all about: Who says you need to have blood to love?" the reverend asked rhetorically.

"Once you figure out what they're talking about and once you form an opinion about what Insane Clown Posse's music means, you really get drawn into it. There's really no explaining how it draws you in. It just does. It's a good feeling, though," he said.

"I feel like my challenge, in this book, is to try to explain the unexplainable, to put into words the feeling that music gives you that is impossible to put into words," I told him. "I'm probably going to fail. No, scratch that. I'm almost assuredly going to fail, but hopefully I'll do so honestly."

"That's the hard part. You look around here and you see people of all different ethnicities, of all different races. People from everywhere. You've seen the kids, the toddlers. What unites us is what ICP has taught us about loving each other. To me, what a lot of what ICP's music is all about is getting rid of rapists and child molesters and racists. That's the underlying message to their music. Stop this racism. We all bleed the same color. We all fit in because we're not racists. We want to stop this and change society, but we get a bad reputation because of the type of music it is and the subject matter they talk about. The interviews the clowns have done in the past, on TV and on radio, they only listen to them on a very surface level. It's all very superficial, where they're not listening for any kind of message."

When I brought up Bill O'Reilly and Martin Bashir, the reverend referenced ICP putting the unedited footage of the interview they did with Bashir online. "They're sitting there with their own camera guy because they know that they're going to chop it up and edit it any way they want. If you watch it, ICP makes them look like a total moron."

I couldn't argue with that.

I asked the good reverend about the Juggalos being a gang.

"We don't fly colors. All the hatchet is is a symbol for a record label. It's like our cross. It just means that you're down with the same shit that I am. I've been talking about this for a while, but I would like to sit down with the head of the FBI gang division and have a group of ninjas talk to them like I'm talking to you now to determine which category which should fit into. I wish they would actually talk to us instead of listening to interviews on the news and forming an opinion based on that. We're not a gang. Yeah, some people try to take it to an extreme and like to think they're a gang. It's not like there's any set leader or hierarchy. It's just a band and fans. That's what it boils down to."

Cadence asked if there weren't Juggalos who got off on the idea of Juggalos as a gang.

"Yes. There's a lot of them. From city to city and town to town you'll see kids who think they're a badass gang because they rep the hatchet. It's ridiculous, but I guess it just makes them feel a little bigger about themselves. I don't know why they think it's okay to take this and turn it into a gang."

Cadence asked if he thought that maybe kids would rather have people be afraid of them than laugh at them.

A heavyset gentleman named James then sat down and asked if he could join the conversation. We acquiesced and James answered, "Of course. That's human nature. Ten percent of the population ruins one hundred percent of the reputation. That goes for black people. White people. Juggalos. That's worldwide. People can say that about anybody. It's human nature to see something different and want to protect yourself. If a man has on camouflage and a gun, he's a hunter. If he's got a Hatchetman tattoo and a gun, then he's a gang member. Perception is reality."

James helped run the club with the good reverend. The two men enjoyed a Gathering-exclusive but very healthy friendship: They only saw each other four days a year, but that was enough. Though nearly a decade divided them in age, they shared a rooting interest in the soul of Juggalo nation.

"With the Juggalos, I don't know if there's God, but I do believe that there's something out there, and that's what we call the Carnival," said the reverend.

James then continued the reverend's thought: "In the beginning, when I first started out as a Juggalo—I'll be thirty-six this month—there wasn't all this merch in the nineties. There wasn't the Gathering, with all this superawesome shit. But let's be honest. It's a business. I have very solid opinions about the business. I'm not disillusioned with it whatsoever. I take the approach that it is an entertainment business, these guys are fricking phenomenal at it. They created their own musical archetype, and it works. There aren't a lot of people who can pull it off. Obviously, the Grateful Dead has pulled it off. There have been people before them. People want to relate them to Hitler or negative archetypes instead of Grateful Dead or Phish or Lollapalooza or all of that shit."

The reverend added, "We've gone beyond [Insane Clown Posse]. We don't need them anymore, so to say. We still listen to the music, but as far as being a Juggalo myself, I've grown beyond what they have to preach. They're grooming other talents to be the next ICP."

James then picked up the ball. "Boondox is a perfect example of the business aspect of ICP," he said, "because at the beginning there were a lot of Southerners that were, 'Fuck ICP. If I see a Juggalo, I'm a-kill him.' Don't get me wrong. It is fun, but it is a business. The fact that it began as a niche market to begin with, and now there are internal niches, is something that's exceptionally fascinating to me."

A young man then strolled by with what appeared to be homemade nunchucks.

"Are those homemade nunchucks?" I asked, as one does when one is at the Gathering.

"These are not homemade nunchucks. I have been practicing martial arts for about six years. I am a second-degree black belt in tae kwon do. I actually learned how to chuck at the Gathering here." Apropos of nothing, he shifted gears and said, "I ate two purple stars. Somebody told me that was the best X at the Gathering, so I took it. I found a bottle of water, found those two purple stars. These nunchucks are ruining my night, man. I was charging through the mud, sliding like a fucking ninja, and they were holding me back." The young man with the nunchucks then saw our press badges. "You motherfuckers in the press depressed my Gathering. I say it that way because this Chaos District was our homeland. It was nothing but a sea of tents and cars. These motherfucking ninjas, they work hard all year to come to the motherfucking Gathering."

With a palpable edge in his voice, the young man with the nunchucks continued, "If you save your fucking earnings to come to the Gathering and don't buy shit to hustle at the Gathering, if you save your money to go to the Gathering you should be able to have fu—"

"But there's something to be said for having a hustle at the Gathering," interjected James.

"Hustling is our nature," added the reverend.

The young man with the nunchucks went on to say that he was a turkey farmer who worked on a Jenny-O turkey farm in Minnesota. "It's minimum wage under horrible conditions. Dead bird carcasses every morning by the twenties and thirties. They weigh fifty pounds apiece because your domestic turkey is not little and they smell like ass and you walk through shit and you get paid nothing for it. I get benefits, though, and I got a girl at home. She couldn't even come because she had to work."

The man was describing a singularly shitty job, but he could just as easily have been discussing the existential plight of all Juggalos who have to endure a humiliating gauntlet of pain and humiliation for the fleeting moments afforded by the Gathering every year. A man like that needs a form of release that goes beyond a scotch after dinner or a cozy nighttime read before bed. A man like that also needs to believe there's something more to the world than dead bird carcasses. He needs hope. He needs escape. He needs something to look forward to. Insane Clown Posse, the community of Juggalos, and the Gathering gave him all of those things.

James then discussed an act of altruism he'd recently performed. "We're all sitting over here, partying, on the microphone, I'm interviewing people, being kind of silly, playing with people. I was good at making people come over. All I had to say was, 'What does your sign say?' Pretty easy. So this twenty-year-old kid had a sign that said, I'M A TWENTY-YEAR-OLD VIRGIN AT MY FIRST GATHERING. So I said, 'Somebody needs to hook this guy up. Is there anyone who will fuck this dude right here, right now?' A chick stood up and said, 'I'll do it.' They went down into that embankment. It was dry. When you hear about somebody losing their virginity, it's usually a sweet thing. Man, it was like a fucking carjacking over there. She fucking took that thing. In front of a crowd and people on the mic heckling him! And I'm there fucking watching, but my friends were fucking video-taping it. I'm not saying it's going to end up on the Internet, but it's totally going to end up on the Internet. She took his virginity like she was taking a car. She was on top, the part that I did see. My thing is I can get everybody laid but me. This girl was talking to me while I was on the microphone."

A gentleman colloquially named Dick Tricks then wandered over to our club. He sported a shockingly bright red goatee and matching fright wig, but otherwise he was pretty much wandering around naked, performing elaborate tricks of strength involving his penis and nut sack. Without much in the way of prompting, he volunteered to stick a rolled-up bill deep inside his penis. It was a stomach-churning endeavor; very few people wanted their money back, myself included.

The gentleman was as mild-mannered as anyone who volunteers to hang a gallon of water off his genitalia could possibly be. He spoke in a soft, polite Kentucky drawl that belied the kitschy outrageousness of his getup and public predilection for masochistic exhibitionism. He worked, predictably enough, at Spencer's gifts, where the baseball-sized holes in his earlobes were no doubt considered a charming eccentricity.

"Do you worry about the urological ramifications of what you're doing?" Cadence asked.

"Big word," replied Dick Tricks earnestly.

"She wants to know if you're worried your dick will stop working when you're older," clarified James.

"It still does what it's got to do now," said Dick Tricks softly and a little sadly.

"How old are you?" asked Cadence.

"Thirty-one," replied Dick Tricks.

"Boy," Cadence drawled. "Y'all got a long way to go."

"If I can't have kids I guess I'll have to find some other way."

"How do you develop a skill set like that?" I asked.

"A lot of time sitting around bored."

"Do you ever shove a spike through your urethra?" Cadence asked.

"Nah, I may be nuts, but I'm not *that* nuts," he replied.

"I love the Gathering," added the Juggalo reverend's friend in a singsong voice. In any other context, the conversation we were having might qualify as a little unusual. At the Gathering, it was pretty much par for the course.

"Are you a circus performer?" asked Cadence.

"I'm working on it. I'm working up to it. I've already got people saying, 'Dick Tricks! Dick Tricks!' It's crazy that this is my first year here and I already have name recognition. I made a five-dollar bill off the wrestling thing. A guy said, 'Hey, you're Dick Tricks. I hear you do a trick with a dollar. I don't have a dollar but I have a five. Will that work?' I've only had one guy want the money back, and after he got it back he ripped it up and threw it away. I was like, 'You don't even want to let me have a dollar?'"

I then gave Dick Tricks a dollar and he rolled it up and stuck it in his penis.

"Oh, honey. That is not healthy. What are you doing to yourself?" Cadence inquired maternally.

Dick Tricks was extreme, but he was not anywhere near as extreme as he'd have liked to be. His ambitions included being suspended from hooks sunk inside his flesh and possibly having horns implanted in his forehead. He'd first unleashed his new persona at a bikers' convention in Hog Rock three years back.

"Let me ask you a question. Do you feel you are perceived as more of a freak there or at this event?" James asked.

"People were catching on pretty quickly here. Y'all are more accepting. Bikers are more shocked. They're saying, 'Why on earth would you do that?' whereas here they embrace it. They want to see more of it. Bikers sometimes are afraid to show their true feelings. I would be walking around and they'd be saying, 'Put some fucking clothes on. No one wants to see that.' Here, I'm walking around and people want to see more. At Hog Rock people know me as Freak Boy. There was a band that asked me if I wanted to run around onstage and I said sure. I would do that shit for free. So at the end of the show this woman comes up to me with an envelope and I'm like, 'What's this?' and she's all, 'You did a performance so you got paid.' I open it up and there are three hundred dollars in there. Three hundred dollars, doing what I would have done for free! And I'm not even in it for the money. I'm in it to meet people. I'm thirty-one years old, and with ears like this there aren't that many more jobs I can have in this lifetime."

The conversation then came to a halt and the cozy little tent became a makeshift concert venue.

A duo named F.Y.F. (for Fuck Your Face, which is coincidentally also the title of a Phish song) brought out an elaborate sign bearing its name before it began a performance heavily indebted to ICP.

A screamy guy with the Juggalocks kept wandering over to Cadence and making ridiculous burlesques of scary faces and poses while rap-yelling of dead bodies and serial killers and mass bloodshed. It was adorable. The closer he got and the more menacing he attempted to be, the harder it became for Cadence to resist the urge to burst out giggling at the sheer preposterousness of it all.

I felt a strange sense of déjà vu. As with the magical gazebo in Buffalo, I was in a completely foreign context and surrounded by people I'd known for hours at most, yet I felt strangely comfortable. I even felt at home, which is not something I ever imagined I would say about the Gathering.

There was something incredibly endearing about the showmanship and conviction of the schlubby middle-aged men who took to the stage to perform under the protective gaze of the reverend. They were chasing the dream against impossible odds. ICP had kicked down doors for rappers who deviated so far from the mold that they may as well have been part of a different species than the rest of hip-hop, and acolytes could be forgiven for imagining that they might enjoy similarly unlikely success stories. For many of the Juggalo-affiliated small-time hip-hop acts at the festivals hawking homemade mix tapes out of beat-up cars, the implicit message of ICP's success seemed to be, If we can make it then you can too. That's both empowering and misleading. ICP has done a terrific job expanding its brand with artists like Twiztid, Boondox, Anybody Killa, and Blaze Ya Dead Homey, but for many of the independent acts at the Gathering, performing here was probably going to serve as the pinnacle of their careers.

People don't become Juggalos because they come from intact nuclear families. They become Juggalos because they come from broken homes. They become Juggalos because they dropped out of school and have nothing else to do. They become Juggalos because it's a hell of a lot more fun to think about a fantastical Dark Carnival than it is to think about your job in the service industry. They become Juggalos because something is missing in their lives. To outsiders, Insane Clown Posse is a group that offers the world nothing.

To latchkey kids from broken homes, they offer the promise of family. To the lonely, shy, awkward, self-conscious, and/or morbidly obese, they offer the promise of instant friendship with a confederacy of like-minded souls. For those seeking spiritual guidance, they even have their own scripture and moral code in the form of the Dark Carnival mythology. They give hope to scrubs the world over. If you go to the Gathering, loving ICP will probably even get you laid. It will definitely get you fucked up. As I write this, I'm beginning to realize that Insane Clown Posse is no mere band: It's Shel Silverstein's *The Giving Tree*. It's all things to a very small subsection of people within the subculture, and a great big nothing to the rest of society.

On the Sunday afternoon of the fourth and final day of the Gathering of the Juggalos, we wandered past a tent where hawkers issued a siren song custom-designed to appeal to the Juggalo mind-set.

"Do y'all like titties? Do y'all like Juggalettes? Do y'all like Faygo?" they cried out to a receptive audience. As Reverend Loki had conceded, it was in a Juggalo's nature to hustle. These particular Juggalos were peddling an off-brand homemade softcore DVD series called *Juggalettes Gone Wicked Vol. 1: "F@y&o Showers."* On the cover a pair of face-painted, naked Juggalettes sprayed Faygo at each other against the grim industrial backdrop of a filthy purple-and-black wall.

One of the gentlemen in the lawn chairs asked a question I don't think anyone expects to be asked at the Gathering of the Juggalos. Or anywhere else, for that matter.

"Do you like Henry Longfellow?" a handsome young man of about twenty asked when it came out that I was a writer and Cadence a recovering English teacher.

When we replied in the affirmative, he answered, "Cool. 'Cause I'm his great-great-grandnephew. I'm a Juggalo and I'm smart as fuck. I got a thirty on my ACT. I'm a sophomore in college."

Cadence and I wanted to support these young men and women in their creative endeavors, so we plunked down ten dollars and procured our very own copy of *Juggalettes Gone Wicked*

Vol. 1: "F@y&o Showers." The hawkers/descendants of literary titans promised titties, Juggalettes, and Faygo. With a pitch like that, they didn't have to offer much more.

Sure enough, *Juggalettes Gone Wicked Vol. 1: "F@y&o Showers"* offers titties, Juggalettes, and Faygo showers, albeit in the most dispiriting combination this side of some misbegotten Juggalo-themed Holocaust drama. Watching the video later with Cadence I was overwhelmed by how cheap and tawdry everything looked: the tape looked as if it was shot in either a vast postindustrial wasteland or one of the nicer sections of Detroit. Any sense of titillation was offset by the free-flowing sadness that permeated every scene. I expected a whole lot more from Henry Longfellow's descendant, but I can't knock the man's hustle. After all, it is in a Juggalo's nature to hustle.

Throughout the Gathering, words and phrases kept reappearing. There were, of course, the ubiquitous cries of "Family, family!," "Whoop! Whoop!," "Magic, magic ninja what!," "Juggalo!," and "Gathering!" But you'd also hear people chanting "You fucked up!" a lot. Whenever anybody did anything wrong, like attempting to set off fireworks unsuccessfully, his or her fellow Juggalos would instantly start in with a chant of "You fucked up! You fucked up!"

The "You fucked up!" chant wasn't mocking so much as it was celebratory. The idea wasn't to shame you for fucking up but to give you props for trying. After all, what is the Gathering and Juggalo culture in general if not an epic celebration of failure? As someone who had fucked up consistently and unforgivably over the course of the last year and a half, I derived some solace from that.

It is in a Juggalo's nature to hustle. And fuck up. And not feel too guilty about it. That extended to whoever had the bright idea to bring ancient, half-mad wrestling legend and unlikely Twitter favorite the Iron Sheik to the Gathering to perform stand-up comedy. Rowdy Roddy Piper was supposed to headline, but he had gone mysteriously AWOL earlier in the day. Cadence reported that when Piper walked past her on the Drug Bridge earlier, he shot her a look of horror mixed with mortification. She said Piper seemed genuinely shocked by this open display of illegal commerce, and I imagine a professional wrestler-actor like Piper has got to be pretty difficult to shock.

The Iron Sheik lurched unsteadily onto the comedy stage, a bloated shell of his robust former self. This was not the man I had grown up booing on the World Wrestling Federation.

"Tell them how you sucked Hulk Hogan's dick!" screamed a heckler from the crowd.

"Tell them how you sucked Vince McMahon's dick!" yelled another.

The Iron Sheik walked with a cane. His once formidable body was now doughy and hunched over. He obviously was in enormous physical pain all the time. He was essentially Mickey Rourke in *The Wrestler* minus the bruised dignity and Christlike sacrifice.

Perhaps the most remarkable aspect of the Iron Sheik's stand-up comedy performance was that it was completely devoid of stand-up, standing, comedy, and performance. No part of the equation fit. It wasn't stand-up because there were no jokes. There wasn't any standing because Upchuck and the Iron Sheik both slipped into chairs the moment they got onstage out of deference to the Sheik's advanced age and diminished physical state, and it was a "performance" only in the loosest, most generous sense of the term.

The Iron Sheik and Upchuck sat down, and Upchuck lobbed softballs at the Iron Sheik that the ancient grappler nevertheless failed to understand. Upchuck asked him about his most famous matches. He asked him how he felt about Randy "Macho Man" Savage's recent passing (he was sad) and Hulk Hogan. The Iron Sheik mumbled semicoherently in a manner that suggested he didn't understand either what he was being asked or what he was doing in the middle of the woods surrounded by strange people in makeup yelling obscene insults in the middle of the night.

About five minutes into his "performance," the Iron Sheik bolted out of his chair and attempted to leave the stage, mumbling something about having someplace to go and something to do.

"No, you've got plenty of time, Sheik! Come back and tell stories and answer questions," Upchuck implored as gingerly as possible, trying and failing to hide the desperation in his voice. I did not envy Upchuck at the Gathering. He was given responsibilities and obligations beneath the dignity of even a Juggalo clown named after vomit.

Like Danny Glover in *Lethal Weapon*, the Iron Sheik was getting too old for this shit. He obviously needed the cash an appearance like this would bring, but his wounded pride told him to get off that stage as quickly as possible.

In keeping with the Gathering's stubborn commitment to

pandering to the basest instincts of its crowd, Upchuck asked the Iron Sheik if he still drank and smoked pot.

"Not so much anymore. It's not so good for you," the Iron Sheik demurred, misreading the temperature and vibe of the room just a little bit.

The Iron Sheik was a professional but he was also an old man, and at the Gathering the old man soundly defeated the old pro who once ruled as one of the preeminent wrestling villains in the world. Perhaps "Rowdy" Roddy Piper was on to something when he opted out.

Nowhere is the secretly innocent heart of the Dark Carnival and the Gathering more apparent than in Violent J's Big Barbecue Bash/Michael Jackson vs. Prince impersonator-off. It fucking killed me to miss Violent J's Big Barbecue Bash the year before, so there was no way I was going to make that mistake again.

Under a life-giving sun, Juggalos danced merrily to a selection of Insane Clown Posse selections at the WFUCKOFF radio tent as Violent J and his helpers dispensed hot dogs and hamburgers encased in shiny aluminum foil at the Big Barbecue Bash. Violent J was once again inhabiting the role of indulgent stepdad treating his brood of face-painted orphans to life-giving sustenance.

There was something incredibly wholesome about watching Violent J feed his spiritual progeny as they frolicked under the sun. If this wasn't Jesus and his loaves, then it was at least equivalent to L. Ron Hubbard handing out turkeys at a Scientology Thanksgiving food drive.

"This is bullshit," said Chris Weingarten of *Spin* as he watched the crowd go delirious for the Michael Jackson impersonator while giving the equally accomplished Prince impersonator a colder though still respectful reception. "The Michael Jackson impersonator has *such* a clear advantage. Everyone knows his moves. It's unfair." I couldn't argue. Death had transformed Michael Jackson into a saint. He was unimpeachable, while the Prince impersonator was unlucky enough to be channeling someone with the misfortune to be both still alive and still creating music the culture at large considers increasingly irrelevant. The contest proceeded along predictable lines. The crowd was respectful toward the Prince impersonator but squealed with glee when the Michael Jackson impersonator performed.

The cavalcade of childhood delights at the Gathering included a Ferris wheel. Super Ball also prominently featured a midway and a Ferris wheel, but the differences between the Ferris wheel at Super Ball and the Ferris wheel at the Gathering are instructive. The Ferris wheel at Super Ball filled me with an overwhelming sense of calm. I experienced the Zen tranquility that comes with feeling utterly at peace with the world and your place in it, if only for a brief, shining, glorious moment.

Riding the Ferris wheel at the Gathering of the Juggalos filled me with the unmistakable, not altogether unwarranted sensation that the rickety, rusty, shaking, apparently duct-taped-together monstrosity Cadence and I were perched precariously upon was about to hurtle us to our impending deaths. To die at the Gathering: I don't know whether that would be the ultimate indignity or the ultimate triumph at this point.

I never got to see Insane Clown Posse's climactic performance at the previous year's Gathering. It was one of my biggest regrets. I would not make the same mistake this year, especially since I'd developed such a strong appreciation for the duo's oeuvre.

During Insane Clown Posse's festival-closing performance, everything I'd found so bewilderingly amateurish about their performance at Hallowicked came to seem charmingly home-made: the seemingly store-bought zombie clown costumes, the choreographed eruptions of carbonated sodas, the intermit-tent stage-clearing "Faygo Breaks" when an ancient Faygo jingle played while homemade clowns sauntered about the stage. I later learned that some of my press colleagues got to don costumes and participate in an epic "Faygo Armageddon." I oozed jealousy.

At the rapturous conclusion of their set, Insane Clown Posse performed the title track of *Bang! Pow! Boom!* while an army of dancing clowns and Juggalos emitted great geysers of Faygo from the stage and fireworks exploded in the background. There was a tawdry majesty to the moment, a strange aesthetic beauty in watching great bursts of carbonated beverages descend upon an ecstatic crowd.

While ICP performed, my head swiveled from the stage to the audience and back. As with Phish, the audience was at least half the spectacle if not more so, and the enjoyment of the crowd was infectious.

In the Evansville, Indiana, airport the day after the festival, I was stupid enough to leave my Gathering pass in the little bowl they leave for wallets and keys and got to experience a little of what life is like for a Juggalo.

"I'm sorry, sir. Everybody that has been to the Gathering has to be patted down and we have to go through your luggage piece by piece," said a polite black airport employee as Cadence and I went through security.

I fancy myself a responsible drug user, so I was quick to toss the one-hitter I'd bought for eight dollars at the Gathering in the trash and hoped to God I didn't accidentally leave any drugs on my person.

Like a lot of civilians, the grim-faced men working security at the airport were intrigued by the Juggalos.

After I was shuffled off to a special room, a security guard meekly inquired, "How was the Gathering this year? Was it less wild or more wild than last year?"

"Oh, I don't know. It seemed fairly sedate this year, all things considered," I said, hoping that I hadn't accidentally held on to a spare little packet of Molly. They went over my belongings diligently before informing me that my hands had tested positive for traces of explosive. I have no idea why that might have been, but it seemed like a fittingly surreal end to my Gathering of the Juggalos experience.

THE BIG FINISH

Throughout that summer, Phish meant something very specific and very broad to me. It meant sunlight. It meant sunsets. It meant manic highs when I felt as if I was going to explode into the atmosphere with joy, and attacks of anxiety and dread and soul-wrenching terror when I felt as if I'd be dragged through the earth and into the bowels of hell. It meant Greyhound buses and overhearing bizarre conversations.

It meant meeting strange people and forming bonds that felt important and real. It meant travel and the Holiday Inn and the Comfort Inn and Motel 6 and feeling as if my body no longer belonged to me. It meant weeping openly and publicly for no discernible reason and feeling untethered from anything but a band and its fans.

Perhaps more than anything, Phish in the summer of 2011 meant feeling as if I simultaneously had nothing and everything to lose.

That is what Phish meant to me in the summer of 2011. The incarnation of Phish I saw at the UIC Pavilion in Chicago couldn't help but feel ersatz by comparison. I was also far more emotionally invested in each show during my weeks on the road. During that quiveringly uncertain period, I *needed* Phish to be great. Otherwise my life didn't make any sense. Oh, sure, I had a book to write, but my brain didn't process that as a legitimate excuse. It demanded more; I couldn't just follow Phish for professional reasons. No, it had to be personal as well. I had to mean it.

I had press tickets for the first time on August 16 in Chicago. That likewise felt a little wrong. For when I saw Phish I took my critic's cap off and put my fanboy hat on. I was not there to render devastating critical judgment on Phish: I was there as a fan.

The tickets Phish's management provided were, alas, too good. The seats were so close that Cadence and I were more or less forced to watch the band perform, and that's one of the least interesting vantage points for a Phish show. What I loved and love about Phish is the grand gestalt: the anticipation and the Lot and the drugs and the spectacle and the road. To reduce it all to a band playing music felt awfully limiting.

I had come to associate Phish so strongly with light that it felt strange and wrong to watch them performing in an all-consuming darkness. So while I enjoyed the dark, jammy show on August 16 in my hometown, there was something that kept me from embracing it with the unselfconscious conviction and overriding passion I had experienced that first night in Bethel Woods.

Phish and their fans had given a neurotic cynic the most precious gift of all: the ability to live in the moment instead of lamenting a past I couldn't change or fixating on a future that filled me with unshakable dread. But on August 16, my mind understandably focused on the night of August 17, which would be eventful for reasons that went beyond being the final night of Phish's Chicago run. If all went according to plan, the night of August 17 would change my life forever.

It ends, as these things generally do, with a girl. On August 17 I took Cadence to a now-closed bar next to the *Onion* office in Chicago named the Martini Ranch, sat her down, and asked her the question that had been rattling my soul since the night of the June 1 Phish show in Holmdel, New Jersey.

In a Molly-induced fit of joyful determination, I had decided that night in New Jersey that I was going to ask Cadence to marry me. I had known she was the one for a long time. Growing up, I'd never imagined I'd get married. My father's three divorces stood as harrowing cautionary warnings of the dangers of commitment. Growing up, marriage was always seen as something you got pressured into against your will. I had no frame of reference for a happy marriage. But the prospect of spending the rest of my life with Cadence incited fevered anticipation instead of dread.

I'd decided to ask Cadence to marry me at a Phish show. That seems poetically apt. I was shocked and overjoyed by my lack of ambivalence: I had to marry Cadence and I had to do it as soon as humanly possible. I couldn't bear the idea of being apart from her anymore after I returned from the road, and there was still some part of me that imagined I would be decapitated in Pittsburgh or lose a limb in Cuyahoga Falls and I wanted everything to be as solid as possible back home when that inevitability occurred.

Rationally, I was in no position to propose. I had just been diagnosed as bipolar. I was drowning in debt. Within a year sheriffs would show up at my front door to serve me with a summons informing me I was being sued by American Express for nonpayment of my account. I was still struggling to write two books I had no idea if I'd be able to finish. I'd lately become deeply enamored of the music and culture of Insane Clown Posse. I was stunted. I was proposing to Cadence with a glorified piece of costume jewelry, a purple octopus ring with rhinestone eyes I'd ordered online after she mentioned she liked it after seeing it in *O* magazine. I was not in any position to make a sober adult decision, but I could not contain myself any longer.

"Cadence, I have something very serious to ask you," I began uncertainly that fateful night in Chicago. She shot me a puzzled look. "I guess I might as well just up and say it. Cadence. Will you marry me?"

Cadence was overwhelmed. "Are you serious?" she asked.

"I've never been more serious about anything in my life. Cadence, will you marry me?" I asked with more force and conviction than I ever imagined possible.

"Yes! Yes!" Cadence replied, then called her mother.

We then celebrated in the customary fashion: by going to the Phish Lot.

I spent the entirety of the show with a goofy, ecstatic grin on my face only partially attributable to an unusually great Phish performance. There is a poetry to the set list of a great Phish show, a secret symmetry to the songs they play and the way they play them. That perfect synchronicity was in full effect that historic evening. Everything happened as it must: An unusually assured "Colonel Forbin's Ascent" segued effortlessly into "Fly Famous Mockingbird," "Possum" was distinguished by a particularly ferocious solo from Trey, while "Divided Sky" and "Bathtub Gin" were both Technicolor, Sensurround epics.

The August 17 show marked the end of one epic chapter in my life and the beginning of another.

I have found my true home in Cadence. She is my present and my future. I want our children to grow up in a world free from judgment and shame. I want them to dance exuberantly at Phish shows without feeling self-conscious or silly even though I realize there is everything in their neurotic Jewish DNA to keep that from happening.

The years ahead of us will not be easy. Life with mental illness never is. Hell, life without mental illness is seldom easy. In the decades to come there will be plenty of bad notes and dire performances, mainly because Cadence and I are forming the Obvious Metaphor jug band and neither of us can play the jug for shit. But there will be off nights metaphorically as well. As Prince has written, loving someone is truly believing that there is joy in repetition: Like a transcendent jam, a healthy, successful marriage is ultimately about discovering the unexpected in the familiar, in finding exhilarating new notes in songs you know by heart that speak to the deepest parts of your soul.

ACKNOWLEDGMENTS

Above all else, I would like to thank my kind and empathetic editor Brant Rumble for having faith in me and my ability to finish this book when I had no faith in myself. Thanks for sticking with me through all the madness and doubt and uncertainty. I'd also like to thank my agent Daniel Greenberg, who helped shape and mold my proposal and get this weird one past the finish line. Thanks also to Danya, the love of my life, for inspiring this book then dealing with all the blowback and consequences that decision wreaked. You are my soul mate and my salvation.

I'd also like to thank Keith Phipps and Stephen Thompson for giving me a job that afforded me an opportunity to do insane things like this as well as my compatriots at *The A.V. Club,* chief among them Scott Tobias, Noel Murray, Tasha Robinson, and Sarah Collins. Thanks also to Michelle Welch for the transcribing.

Thank you to the Maloons. Your kindness and generosity are infinite and all-encompassing. You've really made me feel like a part of the family. For that I will always be grateful. Thanks also to the Rabins, Sacks family, and Gerbers.

On the ICP front I'd like to thank Andi Pelligrino for the excellent publicizing, Violent J for talking to me twice and creating the Dark Carnival, Colt Cabana, and all Juggalos everywhere. Thank you for being so endlessly fascinating and fun to write about. It was an honor and a privilege exploring your world.

I'd also like to thank Phish, all Phish fans, and Jason Colton for hooking me up at Super Ball. I sincerely hope this book makes me a welcome presence at Phish shows and I sincerely hope I did you guys justice. I'd also like to thank Cody and everyone else I met along the long, strange road.

Thank you also, Weird Al, for having the questionable judgment to commission me to write a book about you at the apogee of my craziness. I'm not entirely sure how we got through it all, but we did.

To readers of *The A.V. Club* and *A.V. Club* commenters: thanks for your loyalty and dedication. I've been able to live my dream for the past sixteen years, and you guys are a big part of the reason why.

Lastly, thank you, Scribner. You published *The Great Gatsby* and Don DeLillo, and you got into the Juggalo business because of me. If that isn't proof of both the universe's fundamental benevolence and the universe's fundamental insanity, I don't know what is.